Radical Self Love and Compassion Workbook

A Mental Software Upgrade to Unleash Inner Beauty with Rituals, Prompts, and Self-reflection to Accept and Forgive Self while Increasing Self-esteem

by

Don Barlow

A ROADTOTRANQUILITY BOOK

PEOPLE PLEASING

NO MORE

START SAYING NO
LEARN TO SAY NO WITHOUT EXPLAINING YOURSELF

DON BARLOW

Before we get into the book, let me offer you a free mini-book. **SCAN this QR code** to claim your **FREE** *People-Pleasing No More* mini-book!

Table of Contents

Introduction

Let me quickly flash a fair warning. There are a few reasons why you might not want to read this book:

1. You don't care one bit that your negative thoughts are getting more and more intrusive every day.

2. You're okay with never being truly happy.

3. You're not interested in finding out the secrets behind getting to *love* what you see when you look in the mirror.

4. You don't give a hoot about being kind to yourself or moving on from a painful past.

Oh wait, those points don't describe you? Then read on because you're on the right ship.

The fact is, living a life without self-love is damaging on many levels. Imagine waking up in the morning, and as you open your eyes, the first thought in your mind is how the day is going to be a horrible one already. You have no problem thinking like this because almost all your past days have been horrible in one way or another.

The worst part is, just when you try to think positively and hope for a good day, that day becomes even worse than usual as if to remind you never to hope. So no, you don't even bother hoping. Instead, you just try to brace yourself and hope that *today* won't be the day to take you out.

You get out of bed and maybe try to get your first cup of coffee because that cup of joe might well be your only motivation to face the world today. As you struggle to take a shower and prepare to leave the house, you dread going to work today. As if beckoned by your thoughts, a call comes in from your co-worker, checking that you helped her complete her presentation and sending you more info to be added to the presentation. She says she needs it before 10 am because the presentation has been moved up from 2 pm to 10 am. She thanks you effusively and says you're a superstar for always helping her out of her tight corners. She *simply* doesn't *know* what she would do without you.

As you listen to her over-the-top praise, you think to yourself that she wouldn't know what a tight corner was even if it bit her in the butt. She was always well-informed ahead of time about the presentations, and she rarely did any of her work by herself. She always claimed to be 'swamped in work' and 'chasing deadlines,' but you know that she really just knows how to look busy at the office. She's always offloading her work to you, and somehow you end up doing most of the dirty work while she does the showing off and presentations.

Of course, she never gives you any credit for your work, even when she's receiving glowing praise from the managers. She even practically stole your idea last month and presented it as hers during the team meeting. The crazy part is that you also helped her put together (read as did all the work for) that presentation as well. You know you should probably stop helping out so much, especially because your own tasks at work are suffering. But you're just unable to say no; instead, you promise yourself that you'll help her for the 'last time' and turn her down after that.

The sad part is, you haven't been able to do that, and maybe it's because you're scared that she'll stop talking to you and grabbing lunch with you at work. Either way, you find yourself promising to help her, and you even promise to deliver before 10 am. You rush to work because you don't want to disappoint her – even as you call yourself all sorts of names as you make the same mistake. Again.

Now, this may or may not look anything like your life, but when Trish, one of my clients, started our first session with this story, it immediately became obvious to me what the real issue was. It was an issue with which I was all too familiar. Trish needed to know herself and to love herself radically.

If you're tired of having low self-esteem, of letting those negative thoughts rob you of the opportunity to be happy, to put yourself first, and to love yourself; if you are ready to get rid of the cycle of perfectionism and want to break those negative thought patterns once and for all, this book is exactly what you need.

Having struggled with self-love for a significant part of my life, I was compelled to learn everything I could about it. I have so far been successful at increasing the quality of my life, building better relationships, and finding true, deep happiness, all through the practices I talk about in this book.

I've been fortunate to work with people like Trish, and we've been able to break negative thought patterns, silence the inner critic, form positive habits and increase self-esteem. My work with Trish and other clients like her is borne from a deep desire for others to find the solutions I've found. I've been privileged to see a massive improvement in everyone who has applied the principles in this book.

This book is specially crafted for beginners unfamiliar with mindfulness and other practices discussed. This is not a book full of impressive psycho-babble. Instead, it's a no-fluff, results-oriented guide designed to gently and confidently push you into the journey of self-love and happiness.

If you're looking for a guide with practical, real-life tips and practices that you can apply right away, then this book is for you. All the principles discussed here are easy to digest with a framework that suits your unique needs and helps *you* on *your* journey. Indeed, there's something for everyone here.

This book is perfect for you if you want to start seeing a difference in your life immediately. Learn how to challenge negative thoughts and recognize the patterns of negativity with their root causes from the get-go. You'll learn exercises to help defend against the next bout of insecurity and low self-esteem. From my experience, the right time to start your journey to self-love is *now* and not a moment later. Your future self will thank you for it.

Keep reading to learn what exactly radical self-love is and how to begin practicing it. I can't wait to meet you on the other side of this book!

PART 1

The Basics

I've always had mixed feelings about how people view self-love. It seems like we morphed from a society where nobody talked about 'new age' stuff like that to a place where people seem to slap the term 'self-love' onto everything, and I mean everything possible. It's crazy that we can't seem to look far on any social media platform without seeing a picture captioned #selflove.

I say it's crazy because we still have an abundance of evidence that points to the fact that self- love is still an unknown concept to many of us. We can't see how it would fit into our everyday lives outside of an expertly captured and filtered #gramworthy picture of our latest spa date, latte art, or maybe brunch at the hottest restaurant in town.

What if I told you that knowing about self-love will give you the keys to a happiness so immense and profound, that you would never believe such a phenomenon could exist. What if I said that those secret moments, where you truly acknowledge the fact that there's an emptiness within you somewhere, could disappear, never to be seen again thanks to the contents of this book?

In this part, we're going to take it slow and find out what this woo-woo 'radical self-love' is about. We'll see what science and research has to say about it. We'll see if we can quantify its effects on our lives. We'll discover if it's really all it's pumped up to be.

While I'd love nothing more than to pontificate on the importance of self-love and its wondrous benefits in your life (ask my friends, if given half a chance, I would), I want you to turn the pages of this book yourself and see.

I'm no magician, neither am I some clever illusionist, but I promise that you're not going to be the same at the end of this book. I can't wait to hear about your transformation.

CHAPTER 1

Understanding Radical Self-love

What Does It Mean Really?

"I'll abandon everyone else's expectations of me before I'll abandon myself. I'll disappoint everyone else before I'll disappoint myself. I'll forsake all others before I'll forsake myself. Me and myself: We are till death do us part."

- Glennon Doyle

Whenever I'm invited to give a talk about self-love, I never close out without sharing the story I'm about to share now. I'll give you fair warning; this is not an easy story to listen to, and my audience has mixed reactions to it every time. I'll ask that you withhold judgment until you have the full story.

Ms. A's first session with me was remarkable because she exuded an air of utter *exhaustion* that was almost palpable. I saw the tell-tale signs in her dark under-eye circles, barely concealed by expert makeup and her white-knuckled grip on her expensive-looking handbag. She was a successful business consultant who had risen fast in her company's ranks. She worked for a Fortune 500 company and led a very hectic lifestyle, which she loved.

She booked a session for herself because she'd been having nightmares and loud intrusive thoughts about something she'd left behind in her past. She grew up in a small town in mid-western America to an absent father and a junkie mom. She had three other siblings, and they didn't have the rosiest of childhoods.

She told me a bit about her experience growing up, stealing food from the nearby grocery store so they could survive another day. She talked about staying away from the apartment anytime her mom brought over one of her clients because no one could hit her if she wasn't there. She recalled being bullied and ostracized in school and even by people in town. She remained determined to rise above her situation and become successful. She studied, worked hard, and dreamt about getting a full-ride scholarship to one of the best Ivy League schools in the country. Unfortunately, her siblings didn't seem to share the same drive she did. They seemed content to remain in town and fulfill the stereotypes people had neatly slotted them into.

She tried hard to influence her siblings, especially her younger sister, but they refused to listen and soon stopped talking to her. She tried her best to stay in touch with her younger sister who still seemed to enjoy talking to her. She felt guilty about leaving home and cutting ties with her mom and most of her siblings, but she got the scholarship of her dreams and had to leave. She basically stopped talking to her family after this.

Fast forward to ten years later, she got featured in a top magazine and even interviewed on national TV about her accomplishments and how she made such giant strides in such a short time. She got a call from her younger sister, who was excited to see her on TV. She said she didn't know that Ms. A was so rich and famous now.

That's where the problems began. She started getting calls from her elder siblings, whom she hadn't talked to in years, telling her that their mom was sick and needed care. She went back home and found that, indeed, her mother had a serious liver condition, and she didn't have health insurance. Ms. A was able to pay for her treatments and kept monitoring her condition. Unfortunately, her mom passed away. This was mainly because the mother initiated care too late and her condition was too far gone.

My client's siblings kept calling her to ask for loans and handouts to improve their lives. Out of a sense of obligation, she was generous enough to grant their requests, but she realized they just used the money for drugs, alcohol, and groceries.

She didn't mind supporting them every month at first, but soon, the loan requests got bigger, and the stories became elaborate guilt-trip sessions. She started feeling bad for leaving and abandoning her family. She felt guilty for not coming back home as soon as she could to try to rescue her favorite baby sister, who was now addicted to drugs. She felt responsible for her mom's death.

She began to have nightmares where her siblings accused her of abandoning them, and her mom accused her of killing her. She kept sending money home, but soon her account started getting into the red. Things got worse from there.

As she narrated her story, I could see that she was wrapped in a heavy cloak of guilt and despair. She was a victim of everyone's desires except hers. She booked a session because she wanted me to approve of her actions and maybe teach her how to handle her younger sister's drug addiction.

It was an uphill battle, but I showed her that for all her education and accomplishments, she still fell prey to a common problem. She realized that she was putting her needs last, that her strong sense of responsibility was slowly ruining her life, and she couldn't see it.

She was surprised to find that at the core of the problem was that she didn't know herself, talkless of loving herself the right way. As we had further sessions, she saw that cutting off her siblings, even her beloved baby sister, was the right thing to do. What's more, she could reach this conclusion by herself, with little guilt and the understanding that she had to put herself first.

I'd like to say that she could move on effortlessly and never had any worries again, but that's not the case. She still gets plagued by those thoughts but was happy to report that she overcame them using her self-love exercises. She's happier, well-rested, and convinced that she deserves the best from herself first and everyone else.

Whew, that wasn't an easy situation to be in.

Many would argue that she didn't have to cut them off completely; she could have put her baby sister in rehab and found jobs for the rest of her siblings. She could have easily reached a compromise with them or something similar.

Perhaps she could have. But because she understood radical self-love, she could make the hard decisions to put herself first. Yeah, it seems extreme, but could that be what it means to be radical?

What does self-love mean? It simply means allowing yourself to experience all the meanings of pure, non-judgmental love from you to you. It means experiencing all the stages of love with yourself, knowing yourself deeply and truly. Connecting with yourself regularly. Being honest about your values and faults. Accepting every facet of yourself. Choosing to let your well-being take center stage, not from selfishness but from a place of love for yourself and others. Ultimately realizing that you can't cater to anyone if you're not equipped and well-nourished yourself.

I often attribute two dimensions to the term 'radical self-love.' The first aspect of it is that, in our society today, with its hustle culture and the drive to earn more, achieve faster, and become just like everyone else, practicing self-love is a radical concept. A rebellion if you will. I mean, the entire beauty industry might collapse if more women were radical and chose to love themselves more.

The second aspect is that being radical about loving yourself means being willing to put yourself first, even when it doesn't seem like you should. It means fighting for your own well-being every day. It means putting in the work and showing up for yourself, even on days when you don't feel like it.

Why Should You Take Self-love Seriously?

"Stop acting so small. You are the universe in ecstatic motion."

—Rumi

Have you ever experienced Imposter Syndrome? That feeling that you could possibly not be worthy of whatever good thing that's happening to you? That you're not capable of doing something that you could, in fact, do? I'm sure most of us have.

Imagine you're a detective called in to investigate this syndrome who's a serial offender. You'd have to examine how it works and search for clues to see how it picks its victims. Any detective worth their salt will tell you that to catch a criminal, you'd need to find its hideout, its foundation. I'm sure that after careful investigation, you'll find that Imposter Syndrome is just a member of a cartel, the Self-Neglect cartel.

I daresay that many of our negative experiences are also members of the Self-Neglect cartel.

You know, there might as well be a real-life cartel profiting from self-hate. It's a multibillion-dollar industry that tells you that you're not pretty enough or slender enough, your hair isn't the right color, you're too skinny to be a real man, and so many other harmful beliefs that we've been subconsciously programmed to accept. Think about it.

Self-love is more than some vague, fancy-sounding New Age slang. It's a real practice affecting virtually every part of your life; your work, relationships, body, success, happiness, and so much more.

Deep down, most people don't have faith or really believe in themselves. They are too conscious of their flaws and allow themselves to be judged based on them instead of capitalizing on their positive assets and asserting their rights.

In this world where nobody looks out for anyone anymore, and self-neglect is the order of the day, someone needs to have your back, and that person has to be you.

Signs That You're Practicing Self-love (and signs that you're not)

"Don't sacrifice yourself too much, because if you sacrifice too much, there's nothing else you can give, and nobody will care for you."
-Karl Lagerfeld

Whenever I have a new convert into the self-love way of life, the first thing they want to know is, "How can you tell that I'm not practicing self-love?" And I always say that "the proof is in the pudding."

To be clear, I don't believe we can fully explore the depths of self-love. Or that there could be 'too much self-love.' Love is, in itself, a pure emotion that only allows for the positive. This means that there's always more to learn and enjoy when it comes to loving yourself. Doesn't that just make you excited?

Self-love is more than treating yourself to a pedicure or taking a bubble bath. While those are very nice (and oftentimes well deserved), self-love moves from the superficial and goes deeper. Self-love is what ushers you from that place of constantly wanting to be happy to a place where your happiness comes from within.

If you're familiar with the practices below, then it's a sign that you have a good handle on self-love. If you're not, sit tight because we are about to have a blast.

- **You're quick to forgive yourself:**

You understand that you deserve all the compassion and empathy you'd show a loved one. So you don't dwell on your mistakes or make a big deal out of it; instead, you're quick to forgive yourself and give yourself a second, third, and even a million chances.

- **You have no problems with saying no:**

Sure, you love helping people out, and you're committed to making life easier for your loved ones. But you still know your boundaries, and you can confidently say no to requests of situations that would be detrimental to you.

- **You're comfortable with expressing yourself:**

You realize that your opinions are valid. That your needs and wants matter too. You're not going to suppress them or make yourself smaller to please anyone. You're not ashamed of your wants, and you're not afraid to express them or go after them.

- **You've turned your negative thoughts into positive affirmations:**

Yeah, you still have negative thoughts, but instead of giving them power, you challenge them and turn the tables. You're quick to affirm yourself positively and you find yourself struggling less and less with those negative thoughts.

- **You practice gratitude:**

You realize that being grateful for things brings about even more things to be grateful for. You know that focusing on gratitude even when things look bad is a sure way to weather any storm.

- **You're not envious of others:**

You openly and joyfully celebrate other people's wins. Even though they are doing amazing things, you understand that you're not them and that you shouldn't compare yourself to them, no matter what. You know that supporting others makes you open to more abundance.

- **You believe great things will happen to you:**

You're constantly putting out positive energy, and you're certain that great things will come to you because you're positive and expectant.

- **You practice self-care:**

Self-care is a natural sequel to self-love. Deliberately showing care for yourself is something you frequently do. Taking out time to check in with yourself and nourish all your aspects is something you're intentional about.

- **You're comfortable with yourself:**

You are familiar with every aspect of yourself and accept yourself no matter what. You are not self-conscious about your body, nor do you hate any part of yourself. Instead, you examine yourself under the warm light of self-love, and you're content with what you find.

Practicing radical self-love isn't a walk in the park, and you might be subtly abusing yourself without realizing it. It goes without saying that you're not practicing self-love if you do the opposite of the points above.

However, some sure signs that you need to sit up and take a closer, loving look at your relationship with yourself are:

- **You love to please others.**

You understand helping people out, but you are almost unable to say no to requests even when they are harmful to you. Do you change your lifestyle, thoughts, and opinions just to please people? Do you suppress your emotions and reactions just so others are happy?

- **You're convinced that you can't do anything worthy of recognition.**

You don't believe you're enough and find yourself looking for external validation. Even when people compliment you, you'd rather believe they're being dishonest.

- **You find yourself constantly around others who don't love themselves.**

They say that *"misery loves company,"* which could very well be true in your situation. You're always around people who hate themselves and are stuck in a cycle of self-sabotage, maybe just like you. You feel more comfortable around them even though you realize that it's not a healthy association.

- **You frequently allow shame to be a part of your life.**

You're usually deeply ashamed about something or the other. You center your perception of yourself and your ideas of how others perceive you on your flaws.

- **You don't treat others well.**

Even though you may not like treating other people poorly, you find yourself doing things that push people away over and over again. Even though they are good people, you seem to instinctively react by being unkind to them.

- **You believe that other people don't like you.**

Not really. You're convinced that nobody really likes you. You give excuses for people who might be friendly to you. *"Oh, she's just saying hi because she needs my help with her project later"* or *"She's sitting with me at lunch, but I'm sure she'd rather be anywhere else."*

Which of the list checks out for you?

I'd like you to take some time out to think about these things. How often do you practice these things? How often do you find yourself falling prey to thoughts like these?

Don't feel bad if you're guilty of some of these things. If you're convinced that you deserve better and can do better, then I'm pleased to tell you that you're well on your way to loving yourself in the best way possible.

I'm glad I'm here to witness your transformation into someone new. I can't wait to meet your future self!

How Self-Love Improves Your Self-Worth and Self-Esteem

"Find out who you are and be that person. That's what your soul was put on this Earth to be. Find that truth, live that truth, and everything else will come."

-Ellen DeGeneres

I've had many people laugh off the concept of self-love as a fancy term invented by hippies who have way too much time on their hands. They say, "It's alright for you to believe all that stuff so you can have an excuse to sit around and talk shop with other people. But for people like us, we know what it means to work, so we don't have time for that."

The truth is self-love ultimately affects a lot of things. It has, probably, the biggest influence on how you see the world, how you see yourself, and how you interact with others. It affects your work, your family, your decisions, your romantic relationships, and even your social relationships. It could be why you decide not to apply for that big job even though you're 90% qualified. It could be why you decided to go to community college instead of sending applications to Ivy League schools. Heck, it could even be why you never told your crush that you like them even though they seem very friendly. Who knows, you probably would have been married to them by now. We'll never know, right? (This is your sign to tell that person you've been pining away about your feelings for them, you never know what could happen.)

Your self-esteem decides what you think about yourself, what you feel towards yourself, and your personal beliefs. Having a sense of self-worth means knowing that you're valuable. It means accepting that you're worthy of love and that your thoughts, feelings, opinions, and needs matter.

When you love yourself, you give validity to the fact that you're worthy enough and deserve everything good and right. It arms you with the strength to sit up and ask for more. It builds up your self-esteem and increases your sense of self-worth. All in a day's work, right?

Radical Self-Love Worksheet

Exercise One

We're often too hard on ourselves, and it has been established that this leads to self-limiting thoughts and beliefs that affect every area of our lives. This exercise helps you focus on what you love about yourself, rather than what you don't and also focus on putting your needs first when it matters. These questions will help you gain perspective on how you can learn to appreciate yourself and strengthen your self-worth:

1. How do I rate my self-worth?

_____

_____

_____

_____

_____

_____

_____

_____

2. **Instances when I treat my close friends better than I treat myself**

_____

_____

_____

_____

_____

_____

3. **Instances when I treat strangers better than I treat myself**

_____

_____

_____

_____

_____

_____

4. **Write down five things that you believe everyone should be able to do but that you can't**

_____

_____

_____

_____

_____

_____

_____

5. What activities do you enjoy doing, and how can you add these activities to your schedule

_____

_____

_____

_____

_____

_____

6. What do you admire the most about your body

_____

_____

_____

_____

_____

_____

7. What do you feel most grateful for in your life right now

_____

_____

_____

_____

_____

_____

_____

8. **Qualities that you can find in those you admire the most**

_____

_____

_____

_____

_____

_____

9. **What makes you feel good about your life, and how can you bring more of this into your life**

_____

_____

_____

_____

_____

_____

Don't forget to be honest with yourself when practicing this exercise. Self-love doesn't mean thinking you're who you're not; rather, it involves loving yourself for who you are.

Also, you should practice this exercise as often as possible. And in no time, you'll be able to truly love yourself no matter what.

CHAPTER 2

Self Compassion 101

Self-love Vs Self-Compassion

"You've been criticizing yourself for years and it hasn't worked. Try approving of yourself and see what happens"

- Louise. L Hay.

I was once accused of encouraging unrealistic expectations from my clients by someone unsatisfied with the outcome of my sessions with his wife. The poor woman was left distraught at some realizations she made after one particular session, and she left the office crying. He said she came to me to get a handle on some things she was going through then, but he noticed that she felt worse every time she came back. I immediately had to assure him that day, and eventually, his wife saw much improvement as we progressed.

It just goes to show that people have an exaggerated view of what they might achieve when they start the journey to self-love, maybe because we've imbibed the *fast* culture where everything gets done in as short a time as possible.

Another one of my clients had such an experience. He had become very unhappy and anxious. He noticed that he had a habit of procrastination and people-pleasing. He was anxious because he was always racing to meet a deadline. More often than not, he missed these deadlines and a lot of great opportunities as well.

He began to bury himself watching TV, scrolling endlessly on his phone, and avoiding most people. He was fired from a lot of jobs because he kept turning in his tasks late. He began to develop a reputation as someone with little integrity. He had periods where he would buckle up and try to stay focused on his job, but after a while, he would fall back into his old habits and end up getting fired. His personal life suffered as well, and he stopped talking to most of his friends because he felt he was disappointing them. He had panic attacks because he was freaking out about what was going on with him.

For him, our sessions focused on a lot of self-compassion and self-love. He had to do the difficult tasks of owning up to his mistakes and apologizing to friends and even former employers. At his last session with me, he hadn't been able to get another job because of his poor references, but he felt much happier knowing that he had taken steps to put his life on the right path.

Self-compassion and self-love might sound similar and are often mistaken for each other, but they are quite different. Admittedly, they both tie into the concept of self-improvement, but they serve different functions.

Self-compassion means extending to yourself the same kindness and gentleness you'd show someone you love or someone who has had a hard time with things. It means not judging or condemning yourself. It means tolerating your faults and flaws. It means realizing that you're not perfect but accepting yourself regardless of that. It means that instead of blaming, shaming, and criticizing ourselves when things go wrong, we accept that we made a mistake and forgive ourselves while at it.

We can liken self-compassion to a compass that shows us the way to make healthy and supportive choices for ourselves no matter what.

Neff, 2009 described self-compassion as having three components:

- Self-kindness.

- A sense of common humanity.

- Mindfulness

Self-kindness means not being critical or harsh to yourself. It means being caring and gentle instead.

Having a sense of common humanity helps you understand that we are all humans and are not perfect. Humans are frail and prone to mistakes and imperfections. Once you realize that we all make mistakes, you can view your shortcomings through the lens of that knowledge and give yourself more grace and compassion.

Mindfulness helps you stay grounded in the present moment. It helps you remain aware of the now. When you're centered in the present, you can see your mistakes as they truly are instead of getting muddled up in the past or worrying about future mistakes. Mindfulness helps you acknowledge and accept your present and makes it easier to let go of them.

Self-compassion means accepting yourself just as you are, no matter the circumstances, while self-love means loving yourself enough to know that you need to improve yourself and get better.

I think self-compassion is a tool of self-love that you start with and maintains you on the journey to self-love.

How To Be Compassionate To Yourself

Showing compassion to anyone might come easily to most of us. I remember as a kid, I used to pray for all the kittens in the world every night before bed.

I prayed they would have a nice house with nice owners and a warm bowl of milk every night.

I also remember wishing every kid got presents every year, even if they had been naughty that year. You might give money to the homeless person on the corner or drop some notes for the sidewalk performer you normally see on your way home.

You might even volunteer at the elderly care facility close to you because you know that having someone to keep them company makes the old-timers happy.

The point I'm trying to make here is that, for most of you, compassion towards others comes easily. You're quick to help someone out and always have a kind word for everyone.

Unfortunately, self-compassion isn't so easy for some. You might find it difficult to extend that kindness and helpfulness to yourself. You might notice that you struggle to accept yourself.

Well, that's perfectly fine. The great thing here is that you can always learn self-compassion at any point in time. All you have to do is to stay focused and consistent. Before you know it, the rewards start pouring in!

So how can you start to practice self-compassion? There are a lot of practices for self-compassion, but here are the ones that have been most effective with my clients and even from personal experience.

- **Allow yourself to feel all your emotions (especially the negative ones)**

Our normal reaction to negative emotions is to avoid them, shut them away, or beat ourselves up. Letting yourself feel bad, disappointed or any other negative emotion is an important first step in showing yourself compassion. Tell yourself that negative emotions are normal and are bound to happen.

Self-compassion gives you the space to understand yourself better and to study your natural reactions to these emotions. Attacking yourself stresses you out physically and mentally, making it harder to motivate yourself. A note of warning; while it's okay to feel your emotions, you must remember not to wallow. Don't go down the well of self-pity. Once you observe that you start to dwell for too long on your emotions and they increase in intensity or that they push you to express yourself in unhealthy ways, you may already be on the dangerous road to self-pity.

So how long is too long? Ideally, the best thing to do is to identify your emotions, explore all the reasons why you're having those emotions, and accept they are valid and that your feelings are valid. If you find yourself repeating the events over and over again or focusing too much on how you feel without giving space for healthy acceptance and detachment, it's time to move on to the next step of this process.

- **Be slow to judge:**

Instead of hurrying to condemn yourself, show yourself kindness. Don't think '*I failed again, I'm horrible at this, I'll always be a failure.*' Instead, think, '*I didn't do well this time; it doesn't mean I'll always fail. It's okay to fail sometimes. I'll work/study hard, identify my weaknesses, and ensure I don't fail next time.*'

Tell yourself that it's okay that something bad happened and that it's okay to feel the way you do. Imagine yourself as a loved one or a helpless child. Imagine encountering a puppy that has been kicked because it innocently pooped in the wrong place. Would you blame the puppy? How would you treat it? Would you kick it as well? Definitely not.

The fact is, we tend to judge ourselves harshly, so on average, our judgment about a situation isn't always accurate because of the influence of the inner negative voice. I say this with all the love in the world; you might not think you deserve it, but please, give yourself a break.

- **Dismiss your inner negative voice:**

That part of us always quick to condemn harshly is our inner critic or negative voice. Instead of listening to and accepting its opinions helplessly, challenge them and firmly dismiss them. You could do this by speaking out loud or saying it in your mind. You can give it a whole different character. I like to treat mine as a bad-tempered, nosy neighbor who delights in jumping to conclusions without knowing all the facts. This has helped me get used to firmly and politely telling that voice off. On days when I'm feeling feisty, I even make some subtle references to how they should mind their business and drink more water. This might seem absurd, but I enjoy doing it, and it cheers me up too.

- **Love out loud:**

Have you noticed that whenever you speak to yourself harshly, you never actually improve? Why not try being positive about yourself for a change? In fact, this single practice has created a tremendous change for most of my clients. I am always and forever recommending it to anyone who cares to listen. Be encouraging and assertive. If speaking out loud isn't possible, try writing it in a journal.

You could also try writing yourself a love letter every day for two weeks. Another useful technique here is self-soothing. Pick a calming motion on a part of your body and use this motion to comfort yourself. It could be rubbing your thumb and index finger together, stroking your arm, or any other comfortable motion.

- **Practice Mindfulness**:

Staying connected to the present is a good way of practicing self-compassion. This gives you the space to treat yourself with kindness. It allows you to acknowledge and validate your thoughts and emotions, making it easier to show yourself compassion.

- **Give yourself a little treat:**

I know this sounds crazy but giving yourself a little treat helps! It's a great form of motivation and can make you feel happier. I won't say too much, but the next time you feel like you messed up royally and you've applied the practices we've looked at above, top it off by doing something small for yourself. It could be buying your favorite coffee or listening to your favorite podcast. Try it and see how you feel.

Being self-compassionate doesn't have to be a huge gesture. All it requires is consistency and intention.

Using Self-Compassion to Boost Your Self-Esteem

"Low self-esteem is like driving through life with your hand-break on."

– Maxwell Maltz

Most of my female clients have one huge observation to make when discussing self-love concerning their bodies. One constant desire they have is to lose some pounds and look slimmer. They often always lament how good their bodies looked when they were 18, 25, or even 30 years old. "I can't believe I ever thought I was fat at 25. If my 25-year-old self sees me, she might hit me upside the head for letting myself go."

This statement is one I hear in different forms from different female clients. I'm always happy to help them see that they've always been beautiful, no matter their size or age. When they realize that they are looking at themselves in the light of a lack of self-compassion and low self-esteem, they start to feel better about their bodies.

It's a thrill whenever I see my clients change their perception about their bodies from regret and shame to self-love and self-compassion.

Just think, how many things have you dismissed as bad or worthless just because you regarded them under the lens of low self-esteem? If you could go back in time, what would you change? What do you think they'd say to you if you had an opportunity to meet your future self? Would they be full of regrets about the mistake you might be currently making now?

Several things affect our self-esteem. This is very important because self-esteem is the way you regard yourself. What do you think about yourself? Do you believe you are valuable and important? Do you think that you're nothing to write home about? Do you even like yourself? These are the important questions that determine your self-esteem.

Nguyen (2017) conducted a study and found that low self-esteem was associated with anxiety, depression, and even suicidal thoughts. As sad as this sounds, it is entirely true, and several other studies have come to the same conclusions. Low self-esteem is definitely not something we want to have.

So what about having high self-esteem? You might think that the answer to having low self-esteem is to develop high self-esteem, but you might be surprised to find out that it's not exactly the case.

Unfortunately, most of us rate ourselves against other people and their qualities. We compare ourselves and feel good because we seem to have better qualities than others. Or we feel bad because someone seems to have it better than us.

The interesting fact is that, even though we might feel like we are better than some people, there'll always be someone more handsome, with more money, or with a better-looking body. There will always be someone better. I'm sure you agree. This means that potentially, we'll never have great self-esteem if we're considering other people.

So high self-esteem based on a comparison of our values, qualities, and character with that of other people will most likely lead to an exaggerated sense of self and give birth to extreme mindsets like narcissism. This encourages an almost unhealthy adoration and preoccupation with the self that sets one above others. People with this type of self-esteem are okay with making others feel bad just to make themselves feel and look good. They do not regard others with that basic sense of compassion and empathy.

A study by Baumeister (2003) showed that high self-esteem only boosted feelings of pleasure and made the study participants more likely to take the initiative. This means that it didn't prevent them from harmful habits like smoking or drinking, nor did it improve useful life skills.

So we see that neither low nor high self-esteem is desirable. What's the solution here?

Self-compassion. This is a better way to develop a healthy sense of self without the disadvantages of social comparison and self-inflation. Neff (2009) found that self-compassion makes people happier and more optimistic. They were also found to have a greater sense of connectedness. They also showed lower anxiety, depression, overthinking, and fear of failure.

People who are self-compassionate are likely to admit their mistakes and modify unproductive behaviors. They are also more likely to face new challenges. Even better, it's been shown to have no association with narcissism. (Neff, 2009)

Unlike self-esteem, self-compassion does not compare; rather, each individual looks inward and knows that they deserve self-compassion because they are, not because of what they have. This means you don't have to put others down to feel good about yourself.

Self-compassion provides greater self-knowledge, and since it comes from within, it's always available.

Instead of chasing superficial qualities to feel better about ourselves (*Once I have that size eight body/that million-dollar job/my own house, then I'll know that I'm really badass.*), instead, focus on developing self-compassion for the best results.

Self-Compassion Worksheet

Exercise 1: Making the Introductions

The very first step to practicing self-compassion has to start with introductions. In essence, you're meeting yourself and getting to know yourself better. You may not feel like you're getting an insight after your first attempt but practicing this exercise often makes for delightful results.

Follow these steps to make the introductions:

1) Find a quiet place where you won't be disturbed and sit comfortably. Alternatively, you can close your eyes and focus on your breath.

2) Who are you? What do you think about yourself? Describe yourself in seven words. Pretend you're meeting someone for the first time and want them to get a true, unfiltered impression of you. Don't hesitate to write words that may not be positive. Remember, you need to stay true to yourself. If you have any negative characteristics, note them down and note why you think it's true.

3) Think of a difficult situation you might be experiencing now or one you've experienced in your past. It may be related to work, family life, romantic relationships, etc. Describe the situation as well and write down how it makes you feel.

4) Picture a three-year-old child. She's the sweetest kid you can imagine. She has dark wavy hair and the greenest eyes ever. Imagine she comes crying to you because she lost her favorite blanket. What would you say to her? Say it to yourself in response to that situation.

5) Write some negative thoughts that may be coming to you because of that situation. Now calmly and assertively write positive, rational responses to these thoughts.

6) Now, it's time for some action. What action can you take to make things better? List three such actions. What actions can you take to prevent a repeat occurrence of that situation? Write three actions. What

action can you take to comfort yourself? Write two safe actions.

Who am I?

_____

_____

_____

_____

_____

_____

A difficult situation I've experienced

_____

_____

_____

_____

_____

_____

How the situation made me feel

_____

_____

_____

_____

_____

_____

_____

What would you say to the three-year-old girl if she were in your shoes?

_____

_____

_____

_____

_____

_____

My negative thoughts are

_____

_____

_____

_____

_____

_____

_____

_____

Write a positive rebuttal to the negative thoughts

_____

_____

_____

_____

_____

_____

What actions can I take to make things better?

_____

_____

_____

_____

What actions can I take to prevent a recurrence?

_____

_____

_____

_____

_____

What action can I take to comfort myself?

_____

_____

_____

_____

_____

This exercise should be done with total honesty. Remember that self-compassion relies on honesty and openness. This exercise should be repeated as often as possible. Watch out for the frequency of negative thoughts you might have. They ought to reduce in number and frequency.

Also, be vulnerable with yourself and express any emotions you need. Tell yourself that your emotions and opinions are valid.

Exercise 2

Write love letters to yourself for two weeks.

These letters should be handwritten. Treat each letter as a message to your loved one. You do not necessarily have to be in a stressful situation, a quick check-in, now and again is useful.

Be effusive in the letters and hide them somewhere secure.

Do this every day for 2 weeks.

You'll experience a step up in your feelings and self-compassion level.

CHAPTER 3

Cognitive Distortions that Make for Low Self-esteem

What are Cognitive Distortions?

Cognitive distortions are inaccurate, unhelpful and unhealthy patterns of thinking that our brains use to process a large chunk of the data it receives.

The Cognitive Distortions

Here are the fifteen terms of use for the collective human wackiness. Don't fret, you've probably got one too. For your cognitive pleasure, I've included how to deal with each of these distortions using cognitive reframing.

Cognitive reframing is changing your response to a situation based on your perception of it. If it sounds foreign to you, it's probably because you haven't really observed yourself doing it, because it's a natural part of the human thinking process.

Below are two stories that show this.

"Suppose that someone gives you a brand-new tablet. They tell you that they bought it for you because they knew you wanted one. The tablet seems to work well, and you feel happy and grateful to have such a good friend. Then, you start thinking about how financially well-off your friend is and how you're struggling to make ends meet.

Suddenly, you change the way that you think of the gift. Instead of a generous gift and a sign of friendship, you begin to think of the gift as a charity case or view it with bitterness because they could afford to buy it while you could not. This makes you angry, and you may begin avoiding your friend or holding resentment toward them. You have just reframed a good experience into a negative light.

Positive cognitive reframing is the reverse process:

Say, for example, that you see your wife in a men's clothing store. You always buy your clothes, so you're suspicious right away. Why is she here? She looks up at you and then hurries away. You feel ignored and disrespected because you think that she is trying to hide something from you. You don't want to think bad things about your wife. So, you decide to give her the benefit of the doubt. You ask yourself if you're jumping to a negative conclusion. Then, you remember that your anniversary is coming up later in the week, which means she's probably buying you a gift. Now, you begin to feel happy with her. You leave the store to get her a gift. Now, you've reframed what at first seemed like a negative situation into a more positive and realistic one."

- Source: Better Help (2022)

This is the power of cognitive reframing. I remember a quote I heard a couple of years ago; if you change how you look at things, the things you look at change. Perception is everything, and with cognitive reframing, you can change your perception.

So, without further ado, let's get right into understanding these cognitive distortions.

1. Mental Filtering

This cognitive distortion occurs when you mentally sift a situation and focus entirely on the negative aspects of a situation while ignoring the positive aspects (Hadidah, 2022).

In fact, it won't matter if the situation is an entirely positive one. This cognitive distortion will have you inventing something negative about the situation just to keep you thinking this way. This faulty thinking pattern can aggravate existing conditions of depression and anxiety. Those who struggle with this unhealthy thinking pattern usually see their cup as half-empty rather than half full.

How to reframe:

Mental filtering can make you appear judgmental to others if you allow this mental distortion to get the better of you. **Instead of focusing on the negatives, learn to pause and be grateful for the positives. Gratitude is how you'll beat this distortion.** The more grateful you are for the positives in every situation, the less you will focus on the negatives.

2. Always being right

Ever met someone who couldn't be wrong? They always have to argue about their opinions, and the only way they'll let you off the hook is if you admit that they're right, and you're wrong. When this cognitive distortion is in operation, it doesn't regard anything else except an intense desire to be right, even if there's obvious evidence to the contrary.

I've noticed this cognitive distortion a lot in cases of fender benders. Neither party will ever admit their guilt. Rather, they usually try to superimpose their opinion on the other person, and it all goes downhill from there, descending into the utter chaos of road rage.

How to reframe:

Instead of insisting on being right, **consider that you're a human, which means you can be wrong**. Evaluate situations based on evidence, as this often short circuits the mental loop that supports the cognitive distortion.

3. Blaming

I love playing games as much as the next guy, but one game I really detest is the blame game. It involves making other people responsible for your actions and emotions. The root of the blame game is the cognitive distortion of blaming, which is a chronic refusal to accept responsibility for how you feel and act. It always has to be another person's fault.

The identifying phrase for people with this mental distortion is "you made me do ..." or "you made me feel ..."

This distortion is rooted in the core belief that other people have the power to affect your life even more than yourself.

How to reframe:

Being able to reverse this cognitive distortion starts with **accepting that you alone have power over your life**. Sure, the government can raise taxes incessantly, and your mother-in-law can be an old, bitter bat. Life can be messed up in a thousand different ways. But you're responsible for reacting appropriately in a way that won't put others at fault and you at a disadvantage. And you will be at a disadvantage if you always pass the buck over your own life because that's the only part of life you really have some semblance of control over.

4. All or Nothing thinking

This cognitive distortion will have you thinking about the world in absolutes. It's either black or white. If you have this cognitive distortion, you probably didn't like the title of E.L. James's first book.

This cognitive distortion will cause you to hold yourself and others to unrealistic standards. If a person does something you like, the person's a saint. If the person does something you hate, the person's a devil. There's no room for being human with this cognitive distortion. If you have this cognitive distortion, chances are that you don't give yourself a chance to grow at all, and you have a fixed mindset. In the long run, this mindset will make it difficult for you to do what you want. This is because you'll be too afraid of failing at them and thinking you're not good enough when you're actually just learning how to be better.

Polarized thinking encourages simplistic thinking and makes it impossible for you to grasp and appreciate the complexities of life.

How to reframe:

This might sound crazy but listen; get a coloring book and a grey marker/coloring pencil. **As you color, remind yourself that life has gray spots**. The evidence is right in front of you. Whenever you're in a situation and you want to judge it as either black or white, remember your coloring book.

5. Overgeneralization

I love dominos. Tip one block, and the whole thing comes crashing down with so much elegance. This is the same with those who overgeneralize, only there is no elegance in the crash. When you overgeneralize, you take one isolated incident and assume it's part of a long chain of usually negative incidents. When challenged, you will use that one incident as the ultimate evidence to support your verdict.

A classic example if you may. You go on a date for the first time in two years, and the date turns out to be below your expectations. Because of the operation of an overgeneralization, you conclude you're a bad dater, but you don't stop there. You also conclude that you won't ever find love and will eventually die alone like Mr. Heckles from the comedy series *Friends*. You conveniently overlook the fact that you haven't been on a date in two years, and you'll most likely be rusty in the dating game.

How to reframe:

Treat life on a case-by-case basis. Judging yourself or others in an area of life because of one incident is not really a smart thing to do, as you'll inhibit your potential in that area. **Rather, learn to suspend your judgment and just allow empathy to lead.**

6.   Fallacy of Fairness

Life is not fair. This is a fundamental principle about life, but it's amazing how many people either don't get this principle at all or overlook it when it comes to themselves. The cognitive distortion of the fallacy of fairness occurs when you measure everything on a scale of fairness and equality when in reality, things often don't always work that way. (Good Therapy, 2015).

Another problem is that there are only two measurements on the scale: fair and unfair. Working with the principle of polarized thinking, this cognitive distortion ensures that if you deem something unfair, other people must agree with you or risk incurring your wrath. Another interesting thing about this is the blind spot that fairness is subjective, and what you deem as fair can be unfair to others. So what happens if they also have a fallacy of fairness about the same matter?

That's right, conflict.

An example of this is a man cheating on his wife and deeming it fair because he caught her cheating on him first.

How to reframe:

Understand that life and everything in it are rarely fair. A simple but effective example: lions need to eat, and they can only eat meat. So they target gazelles. Is life fair to the gazelles, or are they dealt an unfair hand?

You can argue that the lions need to eat, and you would be correct, but from the point of view of the gazelles, do they deserve to die just because the lions need to feed?

See? Life isn't fair. Sometimes it appears to be, but really it's not. Understand this, and you'll be able to better approach situations in your life.

7. Control Fallacies

Everyone likes to think they're in control of their lives, even though that belief is very debatable. But with the cognitive distortion of control fallacy, your thinking falls under one of two classifications:

- **Internal control fallacy** is the faulty thinking that you are in control of everything that happens to you and around you. The serious problem with this thinking pattern arises when you rationalize that if you are in control of everything around you, then you are responsible for how everyone around you feels. Needless to say, this is a very heavy burden to put on yourself.

- **External control fallacy** is the faulty belief that you have no control over your life and so you're a victim of fate. This belief easily translates into someone who won't take any responsibility for their lives and can morph into a whiny complainer who blames everyone else for their misfortune.

How to reframe:

As I said earlier, thinking you're completely controlling your life is very debatable. But what you're usually in control of is your response to life's situations. Sure, some situations can be shitty and seem like you don't really have a choice, but even in these extreme situations, you still have a certain amount of control over how you approach your situation mentally (Ackerman, 2022).

If you have identified internal control fallacy as a cognitive distortion, then it is important that you know you're an individual. I know; it's pretty clear. But stay with me. Since you're an individual, you have control over your own life. That's it. No control over another person's thinking or choices. You can influence it because of things like parenthood, marriage, work, etc., but ultimately, everyone can still determine what they want to do, good or bad. If you don't reframe your thinking about this now, you'll make yourself prone to becoming a people-pleaser or a bossy and controlling person.

For external control fallacy, allowing your life to drift away from your control will cost you unless you correct this thinking pattern. Understand this:

you are responsible for you.

I'll write it again just so we're clear:

you are responsible for you.

Sure, a lot of situations in life are pretty hard to control, but not everything is. For instance, in the heat of the COVID-19 pandemic, a likely thought that would have run through your head is that you can't control the pandemic and don't know what to do. It's also likely your anxiety levels rose due to this realization. A better way to think would be to admit that though you can't do anything about the pandemic, you can take steps to protect yourself.

As a whole, identifying what you can and can't control is a big help to reframe control fallacies.

8. Shoulds

An offshoot of the belief that everything in life is black and white, having a cognitive distortion of thinking with shoulds will result in much self-inflicted misery. This is because rules impractical for daily living are the ones you'll use as guiding principles, and you'll inevitably come up short.

Should statements neglect the many complexities of life and focus on how something should be or how your life should be lived. If those standards are not met, guilt and disappointments usually follow. "Should statements" are the major reason behind perfectionism and the drag it causes to you.

How to reframe:

Should statements mandate living with impractical standards. Rather than live like this, aim for living with realistic possibilities. You can do this by practicing the following:

- Keep track of your 'should' thoughts. Write down the details of the situation.

- Explore the belief behind those statements. The most common reason for the creation of these statements is that they help to feel in control. A good way to figure out the belief behind the statement is to finish the sentence with your idea of what will happen if you don't follow your rule.

- Explore your feelings also when you don't follow your "should statement" and write it down.

- Test your statement by getting evidence for and against your statement.

- Turn your ironclad standard into a preference. For instance, instead of mandating yourself to get somewhere on time, indicate your preference to do so (Wetter & Bailey, 2016).

9. Fallacy of Change

You must wonder why there seem to be so many cognitive distortions based on fallacies. It's because we love lying to ourselves, but this is not a topic for this book.

The fallacy of change is a cognitive distortion that mandates other people to change their behaviors just to make you happy. A classic example (again): a wife is unhappy with her husband for wearing his favorite two-piece suit because she hates two-piece suits. Thinking like this is obviously selfish, as it conveniently overlooks the fact that other people's happiness is also important.

The fundamental reason why most people exhibit the fallacy of change is that they want others around them to love them unconditionally and accept their flaws without judgment or criticism (Timm, 2021).

How to reframe:

Just as you want to be accepted without flaws and loved without judgment, other people have the same desires. So you need to understand this. Sure, sometimes, people have terrible habits and behaviors that affect you. You can definitely ask them to change, but the choice to do so lies entirely with them.

Placing the burden of your happiness on them is not fair to them, even if their behaviors are not great. It's also not fair to you, as you'll be outsourcing your emotional stability to someone who might not even be serious enough about life to be committed to personal development.

Your happiness depends on you, not on anyone else.

10. Global Labeling

This cognitive distortion involves using an attribute, mistake, or complexity of a person, a situation, or a tribe and turning it into a label for the affected party. The person in question can also be yourself. For instance, suppose you failed a test. With this cognitive distortion, your thoughts would be that you're a failure instead of the fact that you failed that one test.

This cognitive distortion is one of the wrong mentalities that supports racism and discrimination. A result of a combination of an extreme form of overgeneralization and polarization, reasoning with this cognitive distortion makes you define yourself or others by a mistake or an attribute you don't like without any room for redemption.

How to reframe:

As with the other cognitive distortions we've discussed so far, breaking the hold of this negative thinking pattern isn't easy, but it is definitely worth it.

To be able to reframe your thinking successfully, you need to accept something; **you judge yourself, other people, and even situations too fast, and that needs to stop**. You must be willing to do this, or you'll be unable to truly break free from this cognitive distortion.

Stopping yourself from judgment has to be done consciously as you interact with yourself and with others. As you learn to do this, determine if you have an accurate view of the situation, complete with context.

When you start considering the context in most situations, the hold of this cognitive distortion will begin to weaken.

11. Discounting Positives

This cognitive distortion is an extreme form of mental filtering. It involves an acknowledgment of positives but an almost immediate dismissal of them. This is the cognitive distortion at play if you cannot receive compliments but take criticisms very badly. If I might term it that, the purpose of this cognitive distortion is to reinforce the negative things you believe about yourself. To use a metaphor; imagine yourself standing in the rain and getting offered a raincoat, but you reject it because you think you're not good enough to stay dry.

Hear what Dr. Elizabeth Hartney has to say about this cognitive distortion:

"When people use this cognitive distortion, they view positive events as flukes. Because these positives are always seen as anomalies, they don't expect them to happen again in the future.

The problem with this type of thinking is that it undermines your faith in your abilities. Rather than recognizing your strengths, you assume that you aren't competent or skilled—you just got lucky." (Hartney, 2021).

How to reframe:

You've got to know what the problem is. By problem, I mean the specific situations in which you often dismiss positives. Once you figure this out, you must identify your triggers for those situations. Knowing your triggers will help you be better prepared for those situations and also help you ask yourself why you discount positives in those situations.

Once you know those reasons, you can decide what you'd like to do better in those situations and prepare for them. You prepare for them by deciding on a counter trigger. For instance, if you often dismiss any commendation you get for doing a good job, that's your trigger. A counter trigger might be to mentally picture a huge red STOP sign anytime you get commendations and you feel yourself about to start dismissing them.

The counter trigger will help you break the loop, after which you can accept the commendations and even bask in it a little, knowing that you earned it.

12.   Jumping to Conclusions

You can also call this jumping to assumptions. This cognitive distortion occurs when you interpret an event or situation negatively without evidence supporting such a conclusion. Then, you react to your assumption (Casabianca, 2022).

There are two forms of jumping to conclusions. The first is **mind reading**, which involves thinking you know what another person is thinking. Added to this assumption is the conclusion that you're the subject of their thoughts, and what they think about you is negative. This faulty thinking pattern can become a self-fulfilling prophecy where you act as if they dislike you, making them understandably pull away, which is further evidence for the negative thought "I knew they hated me." (Naoumidis, 2019.)

The second form of jumping to conclusions is **fortune telling**. This occurs when you predict negative outcomes for yourself in the future, often without any shred of evidence to support this thinking. This results in a behavior that is conducive to the negative outcome you predicted for yourself.

Here's an instance:

Situation: You want to find a person to date and possibly get married to.

Fortune telling: I just know I'm not going to find anyone.

Resulting Behavior: Sloppiness and lateness to dates, a lack of attention to physical looks, etc.

Outcome: No connection with anyone on dates, no repeat dates.

How to reframe:

I'll keep this simple; get over yourself. This cognitive distortion places intense focus on yourself and thinking everyone is thinking about you at all times. Sorry (not sorry) to burst your bubble; human beings are too selfish for that. Most times, people aren't even thinking about you as much as you think they are. So unless you have the worst of behaviors, most people's unhappiness or anger is not about you.

To help you stop jumping to conclusions, here's what to do, according to Dr. Katharina Star:

- **Check the facts**

Start by gathering as much information as possible before making a judgment or decision.

- **Challenge your thinking**

If you find yourself making assumptions, actively challenge your conclusions. Is there another explanation that would also make sense?

- **Ask questions**

Before jumping to conclusions about what another person might be thinking, try asking. Communicating your concerns and getting a direct answer can eliminate a lot of confusion.

- **Take another perspective**

Think about the situation from the point of view of an outsider. How might they interpret the situation? What information would they need to reach an accurate conclusion? (Star, 2022).

Facts Checking Worksheets

With the help of this exercise, you'll discover how to combat your negative thoughts (cognitive distortions), which make you think the worst of yourself and reduce your self-esteem.

More often than not, some thoughts pop into our minds, especially in certain situations. And we find it hard to remember that these thoughts are just opinions of ourselves during that period and not facts.

This exercise contains some of those statements, and you'll decide whether they're opinions or facts. Recognising facts from opinions will help you battle these dysfunctional opinions of yourself. Also, if you have other thoughts that aren't on the list, you can also test them.

Statement	Fact/Opinion
I'm dumb	
I'm useless	
I'm unattractive	
I'm overweight	
Nobody likes me	
I have no friends	
I'm a selfish person	
This will be a disaster	
I will fail this test	
I'm not fit for the job	
I'm not good enough	
I'll die single	
I'm not good at my job	

My family is disappointed in me	
I'm a failure	

PART 2

Unleash Your Inner Beauty

I'd like to share something that I encountered once. I used to take some meditation and inner self-visualization classes at some point. It basically meant that people would try to quiet their minds and envision their innermost, most pure self. This self is usually dissociated from your regular appearance, right?

I was fortunate to coach a group of young people, and when it was time to describe their inner selves, a particular young woman surprised me with her description of her inner self. Other people described their avatars as all-natural versions of themselves, clad in simple clothes and mostly barefooted. This young lady, let's call her Kim, described her inner self with long, shiny hair in a cute white sundress (her words, not mine) and a full face of makeup.

Yep. I kid you not. Her inner self had a full face of makeup on! When another woman asked why her inner self had makeup on, she shrugged and said, "Yeah, well, inner beauty, you know."

I guess, for some of us, inner beauty comes complete with inner makeup.

Thankfully, when we talk about inner beauty in this part of the book, we will NOT be including inner makeup. Instead, we'll go deeper into ourselves. We'll start the hard process of knowing, evaluating, and forgiving ourselves. We'll get to know our inner child and nurture them again. We'll get to take a deep, clean breath free of guilt, sadness, or pretense.

CHAPTER 4

Self- Forgiveness In Action

The Role of Forgiving Yourself in Building Your Self-Esteem

Forgive yourself for what you think you've done or not done. At every moment, you had your reasons for all of your actions and decisions. You've always done the best that you could do. Forgive yourself.

— Doreen Virtue

When I think of self-forgiveness, I remember a movie I saw a couple of years ago. It was a psychological thriller about this young lady who was committed to an asylum because she was discovered at the scene of a crime, mute and unresponsive, even though she was still conscious and her eyes were open.

There were so many theories about why she was that way. Some people thought she was a lucky victim who didn't die. Others thought she might have been a party to the crime. No one could confirm for sure because she never said a word. Not to the police officers who rescued her, the lawyers and numerous doctors who tried to get information from her, and not even the different psychologists and psychiatrists who spoke to her when she had just got committed to the asylum.

She caught the attention of a renowned psychologist who'd heard about her case and decided to visit. The rest of the movie is then narrated from the young victim's point of view. We were taken into her mind, where she talked about being mute because she was being held captive in her mind. She had been locked up and was unable to find a way out. She never realized who kept her locked up and didn't remember much about the scene where she was found.

All that changed when she started her sessions with the elderly, kind-looking female psychologist who had come to help her. The psychologist seemed to be convinced that she could be helped. They had a few sessions where the psychologist encouraged her to go deep into her mind and remember what happened to traumatize her so much.

Eventually, the young lady remembered that she had witnessed the murder and felt guilty because though she knew it would happen, she never warned anyone. With the psychologist's voice guiding her, deep within her mind, she was able to break out of captivity and confront the dark figure that held her captive.

To our surprise, the dark figure that kept her imprisoned turned out to be … her.

That's right, her.

She was held captive in her mind all this time. It turned out that her guilt and unforgiveness towards herself for not speaking up on time crippled her such that her negative inner voice overtook her mind. By the end of the movie, she had realized her strength, broken out of her prison, and confronted herself. After further sessions, she started talking and improved significantly. The best part of everything was that all this was catalyzed by the fact that she chose to forgive herself. That singular act strengthened her and gave her her life back.

Self-forgiveness means choosing to reconcile with yourself, forgiving yourself, and mending your relationship with yourself instead of self-loathing.

Would you say that you find it easy to forgive others? You might be honest with yourself and admit that you do find it difficult to forgive others. Or you might realize that you don't mind letting go of offenses for the good of the relationship. Or, you could be like my former self, a tad petty and unwilling to forgive until I'd gotten my pound of flesh.

It doesn't matter which type of person you are and how willing you are to forgive others. Because the fact is that self-forgiveness can be very difficult, maybe even the most demanding thing you might have to do. I find that most people say that forgiving others is much easier than forgiving themselves. They say it's harder to forgive themselves because they have to live with the knowledge of what they've done *as well as* its effects. Being forced to confront that knowledge intimately daily makes the process long and painful for them. But curiously, they quickly admit that it is also very rewarding for them.

Let's take a quick look at what forgiving yourself looks like, shall we?

First, it involves facing the facts, taking responsibility for what you've done. No evading the truth or sugarcoating the reality. Just straight-up acceptance of your actions and the accompanying emotions.

Next, you'll have to express your feelings. Do you feel remorseful? Do you feel guilty and ashamed? Before we go too far, I should tell you that feeling guilty might be a good sign. Because guilt might signify that you feel bad about doing something wrong. That means you're uncomfortable with that action, much like a good person feeling regretful because they've made a mistake. So your guilt might show that your heart is in the right place after all. Therefore, feel free to express that you feel guilty.

Finally, you'll have to find a way to mend your relationship with yourself. You'll have to 'make it up' to yourself and restore your self-trust. You can then make promises and take action to show that you're committed to rebuilding. It's, in fact, similar to you trying to forgive someone else.

As simple as this may seem, it's awfully easy to get stuck at any of these stages of forgiveness. It might be easier just to shove it under the carpet and ignore it altogether. After all, nobody will know if you never say anything, right? It doesn't matter if you never really forgive yourself; you'll move on and forget this ever happened.

Right?

Wrong.

A lack of self-forgiveness might affect you more than you'll ever know. Refusing to acknowledge and forgive yourself for your errors makes you unable to move on from the past. You might become depressed about your previous mistakes and anxious about possible future ones. You'll be constantly reminded of your imperfections– and not in a healthy way. Needless to say, your mental health will suffer greatly, affecting your problem-solving and decision-making skills, two very important life skills. See how big a deal it is?

Forgiveness does not mean you're weak or tolerating your faults and bad behaviors. It doesn't mean that you're absolving yourself of all accountability. Instead, self-forgiveness means that you accept what happened, but you want to move forward. You're not willing to stay stuck at that level; you value your relationship with yourself enough to work through what happened while freeing yourself from the negative feelings that accompany the hurt, like guilt, anger, and self-resentment.

When you practice self-forgiveness, you're laying down the blocks for rebuilding your self-image. You'll realize that you're practicing self-compassion, and your self-esteem will keep ramping up. You'll also notice that you're more positive and even more productive. You'll find that you can be objective about what happened without having your perception clouded by the weight of those negative thoughts and emotions. By default, your anxiety levels will significantly decrease.

Look, self-forgiveness is about choosing you. Plain and simple. I mean *really* choosing you and saying, "I want what's best for me," even though that might mean working through the difficult process. The fact is, you're worth it. So why not?

Using the Four R's of Self-Forgiveness

"Forgive yourself; you are not perfect. Show yourself grace; you are still learning. Show yourself patience; you are on a journey."

— **Shannon Yvette Tanner**

We've established that self-forgiveness is necessary and that the more intentional you are in the process, the better. A study by Cornish and Wade in 2015 described a four-step process for self-forgiveness, the Four R model of self-forgiveness.

The Four R's of Self-Forgiveness:

- **Responsibility**

- **Remorse**

- **Restoration**

- **Renewal**

Responsibility: People often say that the first step to self-forgiveness might be the hardest, and I'm inclined to agree. Acknowledging your mistakes, accepting that you made them, and calibrating your mindset to forgiving and forgetting aren't a piece of cake. Accepting your shortcomings helps you in the struggle against justifying or rationalizing your actions. The fact is, it's easy and even feels good to keep beating yourself up for your mistakes but guess what? That's a total dead end. Taking this first step to self-forgiveness stops you from being overwhelmed by negative emotions, allowing you to move on to the next stage.

Remorse: A mistake some people make is to think that the four R's happen in clearly demarcated phases, but that's just not true. Some also initially feel lost because they seem to skip the remorse stage. Sometimes, remorse may be cloaked by anger, resentment, or disappointment. Other times, you might have to intentionally examine the situation to evoke remorse.

Notwithstanding how it comes about, feeling remorseful is important because it solidifies the intention behind the process and launches the next part. I must mention again that negative feelings like guilt and shame are very normal and should be accepted. They serve as great ammunition for this exercise.

Restoration: This is the part where most people begin to see the positive effects of self-forgiveness. This stage involves the rebuilding of bridges and the restoration of lost trust. Here, you'll need to apologize to yourself for the damage done and the hurt caused. The simple act of apologizing to yourself carries a lot of weight. As you continue to apologize to yourself after every incident, your level of self-compassion will practically go through the roof.

This is also the point where you decide how you can make amends for the offenses against yourself. Allowing yourself to work through the feelings of guilt and remorse is very important so that you can experience the positive feelings that come with this stage. Making amends can look like taking intentional steps to practice positive affirmations every day. Or it could be writing a long text to a dear friend to save a relationship important to you. Either way, you need to be strongly committed to the restoration process. You shouldn't have too much difficulty with consistency here because of the positive feelings you'll experience at this stage. I encourage you to harness these feelings to fly to the next step.

Renewal: The final stage is about evaluating yourself and planning for your growth in the aftermath of the offense. The work of the renewal phase is never truly done because every day may bring fresh challenges, but initiating it is key.

This might be a little tricky because you could be sidelined by unpleasant emotions leading to self-hate, self-pity, and overthinking. A great way to bypass this is to put some structure into it by asking and answering questions.

Ask yourself questions like:

- Why did I do what I did?

- Why do I feel the way I'm feeling? (ensure to name the emotion: guilt, anger, etc.)

- How can I learn from this to further my growth and self-discovery?

These simple questions are enough to kickstart the exercise, and more often than not, you might find other questions coming up as you go along. It's natural, and they should be entertained as long as they drive you to renewal and healing, not overthinking and self-judgment.

That's it. The four R's have been tried and proven to work. Taking the time to learn how it works is important because knowing each step helps you reach your goal faster.

Childhood Trauma and Self-Forgiveness

"You cannot travel back in time to fix your mistakes, but you can learn from them and forgive yourself for not knowing better."

— **Leon Brown**

The ironic thing about childhood trauma is that it's a topic that's frequently brought up and might even be something of a pop culture reference. Yet we don't have enough real conversations about trauma and its effects.

At best, we make a lot of jokes about it; you could hear statements like "She probably wasn't hugged enough as a child" said casually about someone who might be socially awkward and extremely introverted.

At worst, we shut down people who try to talk about their experiences and ask them to 'suck it up' or 'get over it.' Many don't realize that trauma affects a very big part of your life, and I daresay that most cases of anxiety and depression may be rooted in one form of trauma or another.

A study by Wiersma, 2009, found that childhood trauma was linked to adult depression and is a risk factor for chronic depression. Another study by Downey, 2022, showed that childhood trauma survivors had lower self-esteem, anxiety, as well as depression. They also tended to have drug and alcohol dependency problems. A large percentage of them were seen to develop false personas and self-images just to cope with the effects of trauma rather than isolate themselves. Another interesting finding in this study was the fact that most trauma survivors lie to themselves about the effect the ordeal has on them, especially if their parents inflicted it.

All of us may very well be walking-talking trauma survivors who consciously or subconsciously imbibed some behaviors just to cope. Mind you, it might come in different forms. It could be:

- Abuse of either the physical or sexual nature.

- Extreme bullying.

- Domestic violence.

- Witnessing a traumatic event like a natural disaster, war, or a serious crime being committed.

- Being severely ill and having multiple or prolonged hospitalizations and/or surgery.

- Emotional abuse.

- Neglect.

- Institutional racism

- Living with a caregiver or parent with a significant mental illness.

Experiencing trauma typically leads to more of it. Either your experience could cause you to hurt others, or it could leave you defenseless to further damage from others. Its effects may be so obvious and life-altering as to visibly affect your life, or it may manifest in small habits and behaviors that you're unaware of.

Trauma leads to the internalization of faults and self-blame, especially if you are the victim. Feelings of shame, powerlessness, and guilt are often common. Statements like "If only…" "I should have …" or "I shouldn't have …" are common intrusive thoughts that play over and over in the minds of trauma victims.

Internalizing your faults, negative thoughts, and emotions will open you to more trauma. This will take away your power and ability to forgive yourself and heal. Unfortunately, most people are unaware of their trauma or they downplay its effects. (Wiersma 2009)

Healing from your childhood trauma requires a lot of work. You need to identify this event and explore your reactions and emotions to it. Avoiding the feelings will only intensify your mental position as a victim. Instead, forgive yourself for feeling ashamed, powerless, angry, resentful, or guilty. Understand that no matter what happened, it wasn't your fault.

I'll say it again.

NO MATTER WHAT HAPPENED, IT WASN'T YOUR FAULT.

I wish you could write this statement out and paste it everywhere to remind and strengthen yourself. The four R's of self-forgiveness are exactly what you need here. Once you hop on that journey to self-forgiveness, you'll see improvements in your quality of life. We'll talk about the clear steps to healing from your trauma in a bit.

Adulthood Trauma and Self-Forgiveness

To forgive is to refuse to contaminate the future with the errors of the past.
— **Craig D. Lounsbrough**

You would be mistaken to think that trauma is exclusive to childhood. Adulthood trauma is a thing too. It occurs whenever anyone older than 18 years experiences a traumatic situation.

A study on the effects of trauma in adults showed that trauma occurring between the ages of 18-30 years and 31-64 years had the greatest effect on the health of the traumatized party (Krause, 2004). It was also found that trauma that occurs in adulthood affects health more than that which occurs in childhood.

Adulthood trauma, just like childhood trauma, affects the quality of your life significantly. Most people who are more self-aware often realize they placed a greater emphasis on possible childhood trauma and overlooked adulthood traumas.

A common question I get is, "Can adulthood traumas be healed even when childhood traumas are not yet healed?"

Unfortunately, complete healing from your adulthood trauma can't occur if your childhood trauma is ignored. Surprisingly, we often discover well-concealed childhood trauma while trying to work on adulthood trauma. The best results are seen when both childhood and adulthood traumas are healed.

As adults, trauma can look like different things for different people, and there is no hard and fast rule for discerning its effects. One truth that is little discussed is that it can manifest from the standpoint of traumatizing others rather than being traumatized yourself.

A mild example of this is the case of a young lady who's had her heart completely broken by a lover, deciding not to fall in love again. This could lead to her being unkind with her affections to different men, in effect traumatizing them and affecting all future relationships. She may notice a cycle of unhappy relationships and wonder why. As trivial as this might sound, it's a huge deal.

At the end of the day, healing your trauma is beneficial on so many levels and should not be ignored. Take this as your sign to take a closer look at yourself and discover what traumatic events you need to heal from and forgive yourself for.

Forgiving Yourself For Past Mistakes

"Forgive the past and let it go with great gratitude. It will allow us to embrace the present and future with love, enthusiasm, and passion."

— **Debasish Mridha**

I see you.

Yes, you. I'm talking to you.

You've understood perfectly that unresolved trauma should be settled.

You've identified one or two such events that you might need to examine closely.

You've discovered the benefits of self-forgiveness and acknowledged that you could use some of that yourself.

But, you're not ready to forgive yourself. You don't want to examine your mistakes or the patterns in your life closely. You're reluctant to even get into this self-forgiveness thing.

You probably wish you skipped this chapter or were just about to jump to the next one.

Stop.

There are a couple of reasons that might prevent you from forgiving yourself, and it's perfectly alright to feel this way.

- **You're afraid:**

It's okay to be afraid. This might be the natural resistance to change that most of us experience when faced with new things. Or you could be worried about what happens during and after the process of self-forgiveness. You may be afraid to face your past mistakes or prefer not to encounter unpleasant emotions. Whichever category you fall into, you need to understand that your fear is often greater than whatever you're actually afraid of. You're strong enough to do this and deserve all the benefits of self-forgiveness.

- **You're feeling guilty:**

Guilt is a perfectly normal reaction. It might seem like your mistakes keep getting replayed over and over in your head. You don't want to face your feelings of guilt and shame. You may not even believe that you deserve forgiveness. Don't let your feelings hold you back; instead, think of how you'll feel without the weight of those negative emotions, and just start!

Here's a simple, practical way to start forgiving yourself. You can do this anywhere, by yourself. Being in a space with at least a bit of quiet is recommended.

- Find a comfortable sitting position and take a few deep breaths. Consciously relax all tense aspects of your body and mind.

- Tell yourself that you deserve all the love, empathy, and compassion there is to be had. Just say "I deserve to be loved. I deserve to be cherished and nurtured. I deserve compassion." or a variant of them, preferably out loud for about one minute, breathing deeply with each affirmation.

- Write out your perceived traumas. For example, "I'm unfriendly to strangers who seem too nice, even when I don't mean to be."

- Write the result you'd like to achieve, e.g., "I want to be approachable and friendly to people who seem nice because I'm deserving of love and friendships."

- Confront your feelings and accept them. Apologize to yourself and start the four R's of self-forgiveness as discussed in the previous section

Self-Forgiveness Worksheet

For someone who has found it hard to forgive themselves for past mistakes and hurts, practicing self-forgiveness will prove somewhat difficult.

Constantly thinking about the past won't change anything. And, sometimes, all you need to do is forgive yourself to move on and find healing. Practice this exercise to be more compassionate towards yourself so you can find it in your heart to forgive yourself.

Exercise One

1. The situation you're blaming yourself for is

_____

_____

_____

_____

_____

2. How you feel about yourself because of this situation or generally, and how it affects your self-esteem on a rate of 1-10

_____

_____

_____

_____

3. Is your guilt over it appropriate or not?

_____

_____

_____

_____

4. For the next statements, you're going to tick if you're willing, open, skeptical, or unwilling to accept these statements

Statement	Willing	Open	Skeptical	Unwilling
I recognize and accept my feelings and will no longer judge them.				
I own my feelings, and they are a reflection of how I see the situation.				

I've realized that what I judge in others is a projection of what I hate about myself.				
By forgiving myself, I'm letting myself heal and recreate my reality based on who I am				
I let go of my need to always blame myself and be always right.				
I realize that this situation was necessary for my growth.				
I release myself from all feelings of anger and regret.				

I forgive those who made me believe I am to blame for the situation.				

5. A note to yourself:

I completely forgive (your name) _____ for now I realize that the situation happened for me to learn and grow and not because I'm a horrible person. I acknowledge, accept and love myself unconditionally just the way I am. And I support every aspect of my humanness.

Exercise Two: Writing a Self-Forgiveness Letter

When your past mistakes or hurts are holding you back, self-forgiveness might be the key to finding healing and moving forward. And when self-forgiveness is proving difficult, a self-forgiveness letter.

There's a four-step approach to writing this letter; it includes:

1. Take responsibility (accept your mistakes but show self-compassion)

2. Show remorse (show remorse, guilt, regret, or even shame, also acknowledge how this past mistake is affecting you currently)

3. Rectify past mistakes (genuinely apologize to yourself, and think of easy-to-amend things)

4. Release past hurts (learn from the mistake and think of how you'll avoid making the same mistake in the future)

To write yourself this letter, you need to find yourself a quiet place, which will give you plenty of time to reflect and avoid distractions.

CHAPTER 5

Inner Cheerleader Not A Myth

Who Is Your Inner Cheerleader?

Okay, I'm just gonna say it. I'm going to talk about the large, pink elephant in the room. I wasn't going to do it, but I just can't ignore it any longer.

I'm so proud of you for getting here! Look at you taking charge of your life and making a difference! You may not feel like it, but reading this book is your first step to a life bursting with self-love, and the thought of that makes me happy every time.

I don't mean to sound like a run-of-the-mill feel-good pop psychologist guru. I'm not, I promise. I just wanted you to see how it feels to have someone support you every step of the way.

I think we could all do with a cheerleader, cheering our every decision. I certainly would enjoy constant words of encouragement and upliftment every step of the way.

Wouldn't you?

I have to say that the inner cheerleader visualization session is one that many people enjoy. Watching them come up with different versions of their inner cheerleader is always entertaining.

The most amusing inner cheerleader I've heard has to be the one Mrs F, one of my friends, described. She imagined him (yes, inner cheerleaders do not have to be female) as a short, stocky leprechaun with an Irish brogue that always encouraged her with rough half-threats. She named him Mr O Shaughnessy. He was a nod to her Irish roots. He seemed strange, but he did the trick for her, and that was all that mattered at the end of the day.

You might be wondering who exactly this inner cheerleader is. Just hang on, and you'll find out real soon.

Before we can talk about your inner cheerleader, we need to discuss your inner critic.

Do you know that harsh inner voice that's always negative about things? The one that tells you stuff like "you're no good" or constantly blames you for every failure and never seems to have something positive to say about you?

That voice that seems like it's always there, waiting to scold you for any little misstep and unwilling to let you forget your past mistakes? Yeah, that one.

That voice is known as your negative inner critic, and it turns out that almost everyone has one.

Did you catch that Harry Potter movie where He-Who-Must-Not-Be-Named was attached to the back of a wizard's head, whispering instructions to the said wizard? Yep, it's kind of like that. Except this voice is directly inside your head, saying only negative things.

The inner critic sounds harsh and always dissuades you from trying new things or doing something different. The crazy part is that the inner critic is in place to protect us and prevent us from making what the mind sees as 'bad' decisions. This comes from that primitive aspect of the brain that kept our ancestors safe and prevented them from eating poisonous plants and drinking contaminated water. It prevented them from being eaten by wild animals by telling them not to move about unnecessarily to avoid attracting the attention of the wild beasts.

As useful as it was before, these days, the inner critic may just exist to magnify all our negative thoughts while rejecting the positive ones. It causes us to dwell on our mistakes and other negative events, leaving us stuck and unable to make a meaningful positive decision most times.

Sadly, for most people, their inner critic tends to get stronger and more controlling the more they hear it. Most people become so used to listening to their inner critic that they become a bundle of nerves and anxiety, choosing not to try anything new or do anything different.

This may not sound like a lot but staying captive to your inner critic makes for an unhappy life. Living in your mind becomes unbearable, and some might find themselves taking up harmful practices or relationships that do not serve them simply to run away from their mind. Unknowing to them, these habits, like excessive alcoholism, and using recreational drugs among others, affect their productivity levels and reduce their quality of life. This, in turn, makes them likely to make more mistakes. Guess who uses those mistakes against them to make them feel worse?

Yep. the inner critic. It's a cycle so insidious and vicious that many do not realize that reframing their inner critic and introducing it to the inner cheerleader might be the right answer to their problems.

How do we get past the inner critic? Avoiding it isn't possible. Listening to it isn't the best course of action. Trying to bully your inner critic into silence isn't ideal either, and it most likely would not work. Or even if it did, it won't work for long. What next, then?

Enter your inner cheerleader.

This is simply the part of you that comes about as a result of a conscious choice to encourage yourself. This is the voice that encourages and motivates you in the face of your inner critic. This is the voice that pushes you on and soothes your fears.

While the inner critic is a guaranteed fixture in your life, the inner cheerleader must be intentionally nurtured daily.

What Role Does Your Inner Critic Play?

For some people, the moment of truth comes when they realize just how powerful the inner critic is and how much of their lives have been controlled by it.

It's super important to realize that the inner voice plays a very important function in our lives, and it might be more powerful simply because many underestimate it. It affects your mood, state of mind, attitude, thoughts about yourself, relationships, career moves, and so much more. Your inner critic could be keeping you from reaching your full potential in different aspects of your life.

"So why do I even have this inner voice anyway? I certainly didn't beg for it, and I could do without it."

Alex, a friend of mine, was especially annoyed to find out that a voice in his head more or less controlled him. For a man who took pride in his career and sculpted body, he didn't like the fact that the enemy in his head wasn't physical.

I'll tell you what I told him when he asked me that question. The inner voice is like a system of destructive thoughts that make you distrust yourself and ultimately live a restrained life. As dangerous as this might sound, the inner critic is a defensive mechanism to prevent us from making errors while socializing with others. It is originally intended to help us note when we've made mistakes and the steps to take to correct them.

The inner critic can sound different to others, but the common thread is that it puts out mean negative thoughts. Your inner critic might sound like this:

"You're no good at this; just give up."

"Don't bother trying to be friends with her; you'll just ghost her anyway."

"Look at how flabby your tummy looks in this dress; you need to lose weight or stop wearing pretty dresses that look better on thinner women."

"She's leaving you because you're a disgrace. You'll never find love, so don't bother."

For some people, this voice could be sharp, soft-spoken, blunt, or just plain rude. It could also sound like a parent or family member from childhood. For others, it sounds like their bully from high school.

This is because the inner critic develops during childhood and early life experiences. As a child, you were very impressionable and tended to accept whatever authority figures told you. This means that whatever your parents or parent figures practiced around you greatly influenced your inner voice.

So if you got yelled at a lot as a child or you got told that you weren't good enough, guess what your inner critic would have to say? If you were always reprimanded or love and affection were withheld from you until you obeyed the instructions, your inner critic would have a field day convincing you that you don't deserve love and maybe make you eager to please everyone around you.

The inner voice can be formed based on the actions you experienced during your childhood stage. Your learned response to those actions becomes an ingrained part of you and forms the basis of your inner voice.

Gloria wondered why she was such a chronic people pleaser, taking on duties and doing things that she didn't have to do even when she didn't like the people asking them of her. She felt she had over-committed herself, became anxious, and started avoiding the people she was meant to help. Her heart would pound anytime she got a text or a call until she eventually switched her phone off and stopped going to work for a week. She confided in her husband, who recommended her to me eventually.

Gloria said she knew she had a problem, but it just felt like a rolling ball of snow that kept getting bigger and bigger with every rotation. A part of her was aware she was behaving irrationally but for the life of her she couldn't do the right thing. Before she spoke to her husband, she told one of her closest friends about what was happening with her. Her friend advised her to respectfully explain and decline all the obligations, to admit she was overstretched beyond her capacity. She agreed with her friend but still felt stuck. Before she knew it, she started lying to and avoiding her friend because she couldn't take her advice.

That was when she spoke to her husband and came to see me. After a few sessions, she realized that her mother was an old-fashioned disciplinarian who didn't show much affection until the chores were done. Her mother also did not like being disagreed with or disobeyed. She often expressed her displeasure by ignoring a young Gloria for days on end.

She realized that her attachment to those childhood experiences was the origin of her inner critic. Armed with that knowledge, she could finally reprogram her inner critic into her inner cheerleader.

Reprogramming your inner voice to become your inner cheerleader is important. People with low self-esteem have stronger and more critical inner voices, which we've shown to be a result of their brain's attempt at survival as well as a result of their past experiences, which are usually quite traumatic. People like this benefit the most from having a cheerleader, and I'll show you how.

How To Reprogram Your Inner Voice To Cheer You On

I'll tell you about something crazy I did a while ago with one of my friends back in school.

Betty was what I would describe as a functional nervous wreck. When I met her, and we started talking, she gave off this air of deep unhappiness covered by a brittle exterior of fake cheer.

It was not hard to soon find that Betty was conscious of her friends and what they thought about her. She was always trying to win their approval and felt validated whenever her friend circle approved of whatever she did. The flip side was that she was moody and unhappy whenever she was not exactly in their good graces.

She and I talked honestly about how she felt and why she felt that way.

She knew that deferring to her friends for approval and being unable to choose something for herself was sad. But she didn't know how to do better.

At the time. I had become familiar with radical self-love, most especially the role of the inner critic in the journey. I tried to make her see that her unhappiness resulted from her inner critic, but she didn't seem to believe that such a small thing could have such a huge effect on her.

So, I did something crazy to show her exactly what I meant.

I hired two cheerleaders to follow her around for one week!

They kept cheering on all her actions and even made up cheers about her positive attributes. Of course, they weren't with her 24/7 because they had classes too. But even when they were not with her, they sent her messages with positive affirmations and stuff like that.

It was drastic, but I had to show her what I meant in real life. Guess what? She loved it! She ate up all the attention and saw that it made a huge difference for her. After that week, she was ready to work on building her inner cheerleader, and of course, it turned out perfectly OK. Now Betty and I are still close, and every once in a while, she takes on the role of my cheerleader and she does a fantastic job, I must say.

The steps I'll be showing you shortly have been tried and refined by me as well as by other people. The process of reprogramming your inner voice might sound stressful, but it is very rewarding, and it works. I guarantee you.

Identify your thought foundations

The first step is becoming aware of the thoughts your inner voice frequently endorses. Is there a pattern to it? Is there a common theme around which these thoughts are centered? Usually, these negative thoughts are centered around a core belief which is their source. For example, if your core belief is that you could never lose weight, maybe because all your family members aren't skinny, or you've been told as a child that you're not born to be skinny. Your negative thoughts might be centered around you wanting to lose weight but never managing to keep the pounds off. Becoming aware of your inner voice means facing it squarely and listening to what it's saying instead of flinching and trying to avoid it. A practical way to do this is by writing down your inner critic's accusations every time they come. Get a pen and a journal and write down. You could even use your notes app on your phone. The important thing here is to track your thoughts, study them, and find a common pattern. Meditation also helps you to identify what your inner critic is saying.

Take a step back

Now that you've done the grimy work of facing your inner critic and identifying its source, you have to remind yourself that you are not your inner voice. This step is key to laying the groundwork for all the action you will take soon. The inner critic might often sound like it's speaking from a place of truth and authority, but more often than not, it's highly irrational and exaggerates wildly.

Tell yourself that it is perfectly normal to have these thoughts. Tell yourself that enough is enough; your inner voice may have dominated you for a long time because you didn't know how to challenge it, but that will change now. Contesting it gives you the confidence to reprogram it. However, to question it, you'd have to separate it from yourself. Sort of like a naming and shaming type of scenario. Ask yourself these questions:

- What or who does my inner voice sound like?

- Is it male or female?

- Is it old or young?

- What color hair would it have?

- What would I like to name it? Naming it helps you distance yourself from it and evaluate its statements from an objective point of view.

After characterizing your inner voice, the next step would be to diminish its importance to you. This will help to reduce its power and influence over you. This could look like you mentally making it smaller or taking it away from the forefront of your mind. If you have an image of what the inner voice looks like, try thinking of it as a smaller, dimmer version of itself. Soon enough, your brain starts to get the message that your inner voice character is less important.

Self-compassion time

I like to think of this part as 'Operation Kindness Overload'. This is the part where you bring your most compassionate self into the equation. If you've been keeping track of the process so far, we've had to engage several aspects of yourself.

First, it was the logical part of yourself, examining your inner voice and determining its origin. Next, we tapped into your strength to distance yourself from the inner voice, name it and diminish its importance to you.

Now, we are inviting your compassionate self into the mix to help you take action. This involves admitting that your inner voice is there for a reason; to help you. In its twisted way, it's sorta looking out for you. You just need to find an alternative, loving way to listen to its message.

Regarding it as a kind of safety net helps to reduce its perceived maliciousness and helps calm whatever fear it evokes whenever you hear its voice.

Just like a blunt, well-meaning parent or parent figure who wants the best for you but doesn't understand you or can't connect to your person or your journey. Of course, they'd end up giving you advice that won't work for you. But, because you know they mean well, you take it for what it is, a harmless, though misguided attempt to help out.

For example, while Betty was learning how to practice self-compassion, she'd have thoughts like, "You're not cool enough to stay friends with these people, stop trying and stop embarrassing yourself." Ordinarily, she'd withdraw after that thought or do something inappropriate to catch her friends' attention and reassure herself that they still liked her. But, when self-compassion came into the mix, she was able to gently rebuff that thought with something like, "I know you're scared that I won't be accepted because my elder siblings always shunned me, but I know that I'm a great person who's deserving of love and friendship. Thank you for looking out for me."

Just like that. Betty likened that process to dousing a bonfire with a pail of cold water. She said that after she started that practice, it became easier to do it the next time, and soon the voice wasn't brash and threatening anymore. Rather, it became soft and suggestive. The results may not be as dramatic for you, or they could be way better (which is the beauty of this process, by the way). The bottom line here is that self-compassion works, and you deserve it. So go for it.

And Action!

We've done a lot of groundwork in the last few steps to prepare for this last part. This involves changing your core beliefs and by extension, changing your inner critic to your inner cheerleader. I've had people come to me with a lot of skepticism because they'd heard about reframing their inner voices somewhere else, and they'd tried it out for themselves but were largely unsuccessful. By the time I initiate the process with them and they take these actions, they are often always surprised to see the amount of preparation that goes into this process. They confess that they either had no knowledge of one or more of the steps here or that they could not practicalize it as well as I showed them. If you're like that, welcome, and I'm sure these efforts will do you a lot of good. I'm glad you're finally getting access to a method that works.

Altering your core self-limiting beliefs and behaviors involves a level of proactiveness; it means that you're getting in front of your negative inner voice and taking control of the situation. At this point, you already know what your core beliefs are, you know what your negative voice is likely to say, and you've utilized self-compassion to diminish its forceful tone. Armed with this knowledge, you can anticipate its possible reactions to situations, and you act before it does.

This looks like practicing positive affirmations whenever you feel or anticipate a negative thought. It's this action that effectively shuts down negativity even before it gets started. And what happens to someone who gets shut down all the time? They stop talking, or they feel less confident whenever they talk. This is what happens to the negative inner voice, and as time goes on, it begins to learn your positive affirmations and repeat them to you.

That right there is your inner cheerleader. All reprogrammed and ready to change your life!

Doing Self-Care To Sharpen Your Inner Cheerleader

Now that your inner cheerleader is here, we want them to stick around. You've done a lot of work to get to this point, and here's how to keep your progress and regain lost ground, if any.

Who was it that said that *"You don't rise to the level of your goals, you fall to the level of your systems?"* Ah, yes. James Clear said that, and I think that quote is gold. You need to maintain your inner cheerleader, just like watering your plant every day. I mean, would you invite someone to stay with you and starve them? I think not.

There are a few simple steps that you should do daily to maintain your inner cheerleader and keep your inner critic subdued. As always, they are simple and practical.

1. Know your whys.

Finding out why you want to overcome your inner critic means visualizing the benefits of having your cheerleader around. Do you want to lose a few pounds? Accelerate your career? Get into a loving relationship? Be a better mom to your kids? Whatever your reason might be, it's valid.

Write your whys down and put it somewhere you can see it daily. It could be your screensaver or on a Post-it note on your dresser mirror or your notes. Also, write it down in your journal.

2. Find your system.

Now that you know your whys, have a system in place that connects you to your goals. The best way I've observed is to build a routine that works for you. A basic routine looks like this:

A 10-minute meditation with positive affirmations first thing in the morning, followed by five minutes of journaling where you review your whys, express gratitude and visualize your future self.

It is important to reinforce your positive affirmations by encouraging yourself and focusing on your goals. During the day, set a reminder for 10 minutes of quiet time where you recite your affirmations and connect with your inner cheerleader. At night, before bed, a quick 10 minutes for mindfulness meditation and positive affirmations is all you need to round up.

3.   Stack your habits.

Because these habits are relatively new, adding them to already existing habits helps them stick. For example, do your morning routine as you take your morning coffee, while doing your morning run, or even while brushing your teeth. The first few times will be awkward and clumsy. Leave it. Remember that 'Done is better than perfect.' Your evening routine might be done while washing your face and doing your skincare or taking your nightly cup of green tea.

That's it! These steps are by no means exhaustive, but I swear by them because they are simple, and they work. You might think them too simple, but all I ask is that you try them out first with an open mind and go from there. As you get better and build a stronger routine, you'll find yourself adding new habits and practices that work for you.

Changing Your Inner Voice

This exercise should be performed over several weeks because it will serve as a guide for permanently changing how you interact with yourself.

1. Identify your self-critical thoughts that attack as "I" statements. For example, "I think I'm a failure."

_____

_____

_____

_____

_____

_____

Or as " you" statements. For example, "you're a failure."

_____

_____

_____

_____

_____

2. Make a conscious effort to quiet the self-critical voice but do it with compassion rather than self-criticism (don't tell your inner critic, "You're such a bitch!"). Say something like, "I understand that you are concerned about me and feel unsafe, but you are hurting me needlessly. Could you allow my compassionate inner self to speak for a moment?

_____

_____

_____

_____

_____

_____

3. Rephrase your inner critic's criticisms in a kind, constructive manner. If you're having problems finding the right words, try imagining what a very sympathetic buddy might say to you in this predicament. It could be beneficial to employ a term of endearment that amplifies the feelings of warmth and caring being offered (but only if it feels natural rather than schmaltzy).

_____

_____

_____

_____

_____

_____

CHAPTER 6

Mindfulness Exercises, Journal Prompts, and Self-reflection

"Mindfulness gives you time. Time gives you choices. Choices, skillfully made, lead to freedom."

– Bhante Henepola Gunaratana

Have you seen the movie, The Cinderella Pact? It's about this lady who was very dissatisfied with her life. She felt overweight, too shy, and generally unhappy with her life. She worked as an editor at a magazine and had a section where people wrote to her to ask for advice.

So she invented an entirely new personality; someone who was physically healthy, hot, wore a better hairstyle and was confident and outspoken. This personality came complete as a picture of what she would look like if she lost weight, fixed her hair, and dressed better.

She began to step into this new personality to answer letters from people who wrote to the magazine. Because she felt so confident in herself, she gave many women excellent, powerful advice. In no time, her section became very popular, and her readership grew. She started getting endorsements and invitations to speak at events she could not honor because she was living a fake life.

Things came to a head when she was mandated to attend a particular function in three months or risk losing her magazine section, fame, and readership. She couldn't afford to do that, so she committed to a plan to lose weight and dress better.

She eventually lost her desired weight and showed up at the event looking stylish and glam. But, she was unhappy because she changed only on the surface; deep-down, she was still that insecure, overweight woman.

Anyway, the part I love and hate about this movie and other movies with this kind of plot is the transformation part. I loved the fact that she loved herself enough to change what she didn't like and to make herself better. In fact, I survived on a steady diet of books and films like that to motivate myself to become a better me. It was great at first; I'd be pumped up and visualize myself transforming, just like the movie's main character.

But when I began the actual process of healing and transformation, I started to hate those movies and books.

Wanna know why?

Because they lied.

They lied about the process. They lied about how much work it would be to change yourself. They lied about how difficult it would be to start all over again when you fail the first time, the second time, and even the thirtieth time.

They made it seem easy to start and effortless to continue. They made the process look like a series of well-timed frames, with the main characters sailing gracefully through it all to triumph at the end of the day. I used to wonder why my process seemed so long and rocky and even futile at some point.

Can you relate? If yes, I'm glad to tell you that the process isn't some fairytale where things magically fall into place.

No, it doesn't work like that. You have to put in the work, you have to stay consistent, and you have to show up every day.

And guess what; it's not a linear path from trial to success. There will be several stops along the way. These stops won't be glamorous either. They'll probably be labeled something like "Failure No. 256" "No Motivation-Ville" or "Goodbye Progress-shire." It's perfectly normal; it's okay even to have these stops. It's a part of the process. The only 'magic trick' or 'hack' that will see you through the process is good ol' fashioned consistency. Being consistent will bring you results.

But how can you be consistent? How can you make that change? And even after you've made that change, how can you stay changed? How can that change be sustained? Even being consistent requires consistency.

It already sounds tiring, right? You're probably tempted to close the book and give up. Don't be discouraged. This chapter is about the simple systems and practices you'll use to defeat low self- esteem and practice radical self-love. It's not as cumbersome as you think, I promise, once you've decided to win.

Mindfulness

I feel like we can't talk about self-love or self-esteem without talking about mindfulness. Basically, when it comes to positive psychology and positive self-transformation, you can't go far without running into mindfulness practice in one way or the other.

What does mindfulness really mean? According to the American Psychological Association (APA 2012), mindfulness is a "... *a moment-to-moment awareness of one's experience without judgment. In this sense, mindfulness is a state and not a trait. While it might be promoted by certain practices or activities, such as meditation, it is not equivalent to or synonymous with them.*"

In plain language, mindfulness means being aware of and paying attention to the present moment in a non-judgmental manner. You could say that mindfulness simply means being conscious of the present.

It's important because it's a great way to connect with yourself, calm yourself, and positively influence your thoughts and emotions. Mindfulness has a lot of benefits. Some of these benefits include:

- Significant stress reduction

- A reduction in anxiety and depressive symptoms.

- A lower likelihood of burnout and tiredness.

Mindful Breathing

Mindful breathing is a huge part of the practice of mindfulness and is great for your heart health (Malhotra 2021), helps to reduce anxiety (Chen 2016), reduces stress (Hopper 2018) and can even be used as a treatment for symptoms of depression and other emotional disorders (Jerath, 2015).

These mindful breathing exercises are simple and practical. They are a great way to achieve self-love and increased self-esteem through self-compassion.

1) Basic Mindful Breathing Routine.

This simple routine can be practiced in the morning or evening and only takes five to seven minutes of your time. All you need is a quiet place that is comfortable to sit or lie in. This is perfect for beginners and still relevant for intermediate or advanced-level mindfulness practitioners. Follow this step-by-step process

- Pick a quiet, comfortable place where you can sit or lie down.

- Keep your eyes closed and take a few deep breaths.

- Relax each muscle group in your body consciously, one-by-one. Start with your face, neck, arms, chest, etc.

- Start by observing your breath … notice how your chest and belly expand when you breathe in and how they contract when you breathe out.

- Keep your focus on your breathing and remain aware of your breath pattern.

- Your mind is bound to wander; if this happens, gently take note of it and bring your mind back as softly as possible,

- Remain aware of your breath and keep your focus on your breathing patterns.

- After five minutes of focused breathing, gently prepare yourself to exit this mindful breathing session while thinking about how relaxed and calm you feel.

- Express gratitude to yourself for participating in this exercise.

2) **Mindful breathing for stress relief, overthinking, and breaking the hold of the inner critic.**

This routine is helpful for quick stress relief. It can also be used to calm the mind that's overthinking or in the grip of a particularly strong negative thought pattern. This exercise can be done in as little as two minutes and used in emergencies.

- Close your eyes in a quiet room and observe your breath.

- Stay focused on your breath pattern and gently guide your mind when it wanders.

- Breathe slowly for two counts.

- Breathe out slowly for four counts.

- Repeat this as often as possible for two to five minutes.

This mindful breathing technique focuses on a longer exhale, which activates the Parasympathetic Nervous System (PNS). The PNS is involved in relaxing the body, so this means a reduction in heart rate, blood pressure, and respiratory rate.

Mindful Awareness

This simply involves being immersed in the present moment while identifying your feelings and thoughts in that moment. This exercise helps you observe the events of life impartially.

It is very beneficial to you and helps calm your mind down. Simply observing each moment as it comes and your thoughts and feelings at that moment without judgment allows you to let go of the regular worries and activities your mind has.

Now, you can breathe easy while your mind is blessedly calm and quiet, allowing your soul some solitude and peace. Connecting with yourself in these quiet, blissful moments of mindful awareness is often profound.

How to practice mindful awareness:

- Set aside fifteen mins to intentionally practice mindfulness.

- You don't need to close your eyes or isolate yourself; rather, focus on whatever activity you're carrying out.

- Avoid the distraction and buzz around you. Choose to be present in every aspect of that activity.

- Give your full attention to one activity or task instead of multi-tasking. A good example of such an activity would be taking a walk and noting the environment, the crisp air, the smell of flowers, and the color of the sky, noticing the thoughts and emotions that float through your head while you're focused on the present.

- Instead of holding on to these thoughts, observe them and let them drift away, taking their attendant worries and anxieties with them.

- You can repeat this as often as you like but for best results, pair it with an activity that's already a habit, like taking your morning coffee or walking to your favorite café for your lunch break.

Journaling

Journaling might very well be one of the most underrated practices. I recommend it to everyone. Most of them can't believe that an empty notepad and a pen can make such a drastic difference in their lives.

Journaling will help you track your thought patterns, mood, and progression through each stage of your self-development journey. It will help you process negative emotions in a non-judgmental, safe space. It helps to reduce your stress levels.

Trust me, offloading your worries and troubling emotions onto a blank page will do a lot for you. It will help you speak positively to yourself and will allow you to tackle negative self-thoughts and behaviors objectively. Look, the benefits of journaling are too much to gush about. Just do it. You'll thank me later.

Gratitude Prompts

What does it mean to express gratitude, and why is it so important? I believe that unhappiness can be largely defeated by expressing gratitude. Gratitude simply means being thankful for what you have at the moment while being positive about your current situations.

Expressing gratitude helps you eliminate your negative emotions by focusing solely on the positive aspects of your life. It also directly increases your happiness and self-esteem. You'll be able to sleep better and face tough situations with a natural resilience and the certainty that things will get better at the end of the day.

A huge advantage of practicing gratitude is that it improves your social relationships. When you think about things you're grateful for, you start to realize and better appreciate what people around you have done for you or what they mean to you. This leads you to express gratitude to them more often than before. This, in turn, strengthens your relationship with them and makes them appreciate you more.

A good way to practice gratitude is to write what you're grateful for in a gratitude journal. As always, the best way to make this a habit that sticks is to do it alongside your habits. You can choose to treat the prompts below as questions that you could answer one by one, every day. You can also keep answering whichever ones you like and can identify with. As long as you consistently practice gratitude in your journal, you're doing an amazing job.

Writing in your gratitude journal doesn't have to be complicated; here are some prompts to get you started.

Gratitude Journal Prompts:

- Write five things you're grateful for.

- Write five things you're good at.

- What five personal qualities do you like about yourself?

- What's your favorite holiday and why?

- What's your favorite TV show and why?

- What's your favorite sports team and why?

- What kinds of movies do you enjoy and why?

- Write about someone you can always rely on for help.

- Who made you smile today?

- What event made you smile today?

- How can you make someone smile today?

- Write about someone who makes your life better

- What do you own that makes your life easier?

- Name one place that you're grateful for. Why are you grateful for this place?

- Write about a happy memory.

- What do you like the most about your family?

- What is a weird family tradition that you absolutely adore?

- How did you turn a negative moment into a positive one?

Morning and Evening Journaling

Writing in your journal every morning is a great way to get your thoughts organized and set your mood and intentions for the day. You can choose to journal either in the morning or at night. I recommend doing it both in the morning and at night.

Here are some prompts to help take charge of your mornings:

- What are you grateful for today?

- What do you want to accomplish today?

- What kept you up last night?

- Today, what five things must you accomplish?

- What parts of your life do you want to improve?

- What are you most proud of?

- If you could do one small thing today to move you in the direction of your goals, what would it be?

- What about your current situation would make your childhood self amazed right now?

Evening prompts

- What's one thing you learned from today?

- How do you feel right now?

- What thoughts are hard for you to let go of right now?

- What went well for you today?

- What was the biggest challenge you faced today?

- What potential bad situation could you have encountered today that you didn't?

- What are five things you're grateful for today?

- What must you achieve tomorrow?

- What do you want to dream about tonight?

- What are you looking forward to tomorrow?

- What do you want to take from today to tomorrow?

Self- reflection Exercises

Socrates said that *"an unexamined life isn't worth living,"* and I agree. Self-reflection is a tool we must regularly utilize on our journey to self-love. It shouldn't only be brought out at the end of the year or at the beginning of the new year.

I recommend a monthly self-reflection exercise in general; however, you might need to do it on a daily or weekly basis. But the intervals between each self-reflection session should not exceed a month for best results.

Try this simple self-reflection exercise:

- At the beginning of your day, write down one major thing you need to achieve today to get you closer to your goal.

- Then write down the potential deterrents to your achieving that one thing.

- Now, write what you can do to avoid those deterrents and how to overcome them if they occur.

At the end of your day,

- Reflect on the day's events and write what you've learned about yourself during the day.

This basic exercise is great for a routine daily or weekly check. However, before you start doing a routine exercise, you need to do a major session where you examine key areas of your life to decide how to achieve your goals. The worksheet below is a clear guide on how a major session should go. Feel free to add other questions as necessary.

Self-reflection Worksheet.

This can be done in about thirty minutes to one hour. However, feel free to do this exercise in smaller chunks of time.

101

1) What are the things that are important to you?

_____
_____
_____
_____
_____
_____

2) Has that changed in recent times? If so, how has it changed?

_____
_____
_____
_____
_____
_____
_____

3) How are you coordinating your actions to achieve those things that are important to you?

_____
_____
_____
_____
_____
_____

4) Are you satisfied with your attempts so far?

_____

_____

_____

_____

_____

_____

_____

5) What else can you do to achieve your important goals?

_____

_____

_____

_____

_____

_____

_____

6) What does your ideal life look like? (be as explicit as possible)

_____

_____

_____

_____

_____

_____

_____

7) What are the five most important things in your life (e.g. family, career, fitness, etc.)

_____

_____

_____

_____

_____

_____

_____

8) In order of the time spent on each one, from the most time spent to the least time spent, rearrange the list you itemized in no. 7

_____

_____

_____

_____

_____

_____

_____

9) Examine your new list. Are you satisfied? If yes, why?

_____

_____

_____

_____

_____

_____

10) If not, what would you change?

_____

_____

_____

_____

_____

_____

_____

11) What would you tell your children never to do?

_____

_____

_____

_____

_____

_____

12) What would you advise your children to do?

_____

_____

_____

_____

_____

_____

_____

13) Describe yourself in three words.

_____

_____

_____

_____

_____

_____

14) What scares you?

_____

_____

_____

_____

_____

_____

15) What are your biggest strengths?

_____

_____

_____

_____

_____

_____

16) What are your biggest weaknesses?

_____

_____

_____

_____

_____

_____

_____

17) What are you feeling right now?

_____

_____

_____

_____

_____

_____

18) What actions/events are making you feel this way?

_____

_____

_____

_____

_____

_____

_____

19) How do these feelings affect you?

_____

_____

_____

_____

_____

_____

_____

20) What support do you need to work through these feelings?

_____

_____

_____

_____

_____

_____

_____

These questions should be periodically answered, and your growth through each phase will be easily evident here. You can count on that.

PART 3

Effective Self-care

Ted is one of my friends who started being intentional about self-care a little while ago. When I asked him what he thought about self-care, he said, and I quote:

"It's the best part. It's like hiking for a full day across a treacherous mountain and finally getting to the lodge at the foot of the mountain. It's like taking a cool shower to wash off the dirt and sweat of the hike. It's like coming home, taking a glass of cold water on a hot day, and letting out a huge sigh of relief."

I've never thought about self-care in those terms before. But Ted? He hit the nail on the head. Precisely. I don't think there's a more profound way to describe self-care, do you? I would actually love to hear from you; what does self-care mean to you? You can drop a comment on Amazon or shoot me a mail anytime. I can't wait to hear from you and read all about what self- care means to you.

I don't mean to sound like an old stick-in-the-mud, but just doing 'self-care' is not the same as doing *Effective Self-Care*. In the first place, the concept of self-care has been relegated to spa appointments, shopping trips, and staycations. There's more to it than that. A whole lot more. In this part, we'll look at what effective self-care means and its benefits. We'll also find out how we can truly practice self-care. Oh, and you'll get to see my magic trick! I know I said I wasn't a magician earlier, but what if I was just a teensy bit? Oh, go look for yourself!

CHAPTER 7

Self-care Rituals for a Healthy Self-esteem

My friend Toby didn't have the best experience growing up. It was extremely difficult for him because he was a shy kid. This shyness probably developed from the need to insulate himself from his guardians' constant arguments. His uncle and his wife never had a cordial relationship. Unfortunately, he was the recipient of the transferred aggression from his aunt. She lashed out at any given opportunity, and as a child, he could never defend himself. He grew up to become a timid person and also a loner. He preferred being ignored and was most comfortable by himself.

Sadly, he wasn't very confident, and he soon became depressed. At this point, he realized that he needed help. He found out that wallowing in his past only took away his power and that he didn't have to be perfect to be accepted. After this epiphany, he found it much easier to forgive himself and to embrace healing. His healing led him to discover that he couldn't control what people said or did, but he could control the way he reacted. This was the takeoff point for the most significant part of his healing process.

– Lois

We often can't quantify the effect our past has on us until we deliberately try to look into the future. One big mistake I think we've all been conditioned to make is disregarding the components that make us who we are. Our childhood, the parenting styles we experienced growing up, or even the fact that we experienced one form of trauma or the other. This is why I applaud anyone who's self-aware enough to see that they need help and bold enough to go for it.

Like you.

Yes, you. Grabbing this book, to you, might just seem like an ordinary gesture or maybe a whim but trust me, it's a sign that your soul can't settle for less. That's why you're here now, trying to become the best possible version of yourself, and I honor that.

Whew! That was a little intense. But I just had to say it.

Let's get back to it.

Confronting negative thoughts and letting yourself experience self-forgiveness is often underestimated. It's something so important and needful; we all, at some point, need that dose of self-forgiveness. It's the way to go if you wish to catapult yourself from the murky terrain of low self-esteem and onto a beautiful journey toward achieving self-esteem.

You could compare the journey of building up your self-esteem to a chess game. While it's possible to win a game by dumb luck, having a winning strategy is almost a guarantee of success. I say 'almost' here because the knowledge of this strategy is useless without consistent execution. To build healthy self-esteem, you need to make a move. You need to take action. But you just can't stop there; you need to keep making consistent moves. A daily routine soon develops into a habit, and good habits are the key to transformation.

I can almost hear you saying, "Oh, I don't have time to start a daily routine. I can't trust that I'll be consistent." Well, guess what? You already have a daily routine, and it consists of those things you do every day. Simple. If you wake up every day to scroll on your phone, or you'd rather have pop-tarts for breakfast instead of a healthy meal, or you'd prefer to sleep in rather than work out every morning, that's your routine. So you *can* sustain a routine, just not a good one. The question is, how badly do you want an improvement in your life?

Wait, did I say improvement? Nah. These self-care rituals won't give your life an ordinary improvement. They'll give it a complete overhaul of positivity and power. You'll take complete charge of your life and find yourself getting ahead in leaps and bounds. Yeah, that way. That's what I wanted to say.

Consistently practicing self-care rituals will boost your self-esteem. They'll help you achieve super-duper self-esteem that doesn't get crushed by anything. Your self-love and confidence will experience a revival if you're consistent.

I'll go on from here to discuss six extremely important self-care rituals that you will find helpful on this journey. They are:

1. Journaling

2. Meditation

3. Affirmations

4. Gratitude

5. Physical exercise

6. Getting Support from Support Groups.

So let's pick them one after the other and discuss them.

1. Journaling

Journaling is the act of penning down your thoughts, events, and experiences openly and honestly. Your journal is a safe place to rant and express your feelings without reservation. It is a safe haven where you can be vulnerable without judgment. It's not a surprise that some journals are guarded and encrypted. It's a great way to process your thoughts, experiences, or feelings. I daresay that the closure you often pursue can be found within the pages of your journal.

Keeping a journal builds and boosts a healthy self-esteem because the process helps you to relive your experiences and pen down your thoughts. The act of writing down these experiences is often therapeutic, and it helps to heal you from pain, anger, and resentment. Journaling helps you dig into your true feelings and bring them into perspective. It allows you to revisit your entries, assess how much you have grown, and relive beautiful memories that make you feel good.

There are no hard and fast rules about your approach to journaling. Just do what works best for you; this could mean using a pen and paper or an e-journal. You can also make use of recording devices to document your thoughts and emotions.

I can almost feel you getting tense and trying to make this complicated. Relax! The only thing to keep in mind here is that the essence of journaling is to help you put down your thoughts. That's it. Some other benefits are:

- Writing about your feelings is linked to decreased mental distress.

- Writing about an emotional event can help you break away from the nonstop cycle of obsessively thinking over what happened.

- Writing privately about a stressful event could give you the courage to reach out for social support. This can help with emotional healing.

- Writing down your feelings about a difficult situation can help you understand it better. The act of putting an experience into words and structure allows you to form new perceptions about events.

You can use any device or method you want. Just make sure that it is easily accessible and convenient for that purpose.

Helpful Tips on Journaling

Getting started on the journaling journey can be overwhelming. These tips will make the process easier:

- **Pick a time.**

Have a set time for journaling but be flexible. As you are keeping a record of your thoughts and emotions, you may want to do this in private. Sticking to a particular time and day is recommended because on the one hand, it helps build consistency. Being consistent does not mean you have to journal every day. It means understanding the dynamics that work for you and sticking to it. If that means that you journal only on Saturday mornings, that's absolutely fine. On the other hand, keeping to this practice shows that you can keep your word to yourself, which increases your self-confidence and boosts your self-esteem.

- **Journal at your own pace.**

No schedule dictates when and how you should keep your journal. Stick to what works for you. Journaling at your pace is therapeutic because you write/record when you are comfortable doing so.

- **Keep it simple.**

Since this is your personal account, you don't need to be overly serious with your writing. You may not be obligated to follow the strict grammar or sentence structure rules. Keeping it simple gives full expression to your thoughts.

- **Be truthful about your feelings, and don't hold anything back.**

The process of building healthy self-esteem requires truthfulness. You need to be truthful with yourself. Write the way you feel or perceive a thing. Write your truth unashamedly, for it is in this process that you find true healing.

Getting started on journaling might appear daunting, especially if you are not used to it. But the ripple effect it has on your self-esteem makes it worthwhile. Journaling helps you unravel your suppressed emotions and feelings. It's like a time machine that helps you go back in time to address the root of your low self-esteem with the sole aim of bringing complete healing. This is why you have to be truthful with yourself in this process. By being truthful, you give yourself the permission to forgive, heal, and set yourself free from the shackles of low self-esteem.

Journal Prompts and their Uses

To make the most of your journaling experience, you may need to use some journal prompts to boost your self-confidence. Journal prompts, also known as writing prompts, are journaling ideas that help you to focus on what to write. Using journal prompts gives you a clearer direction before you start writing.

Below are helpful prompts that can get you started on your journaling journey:

- What does the word 'confidence' mean to you?

- What has been the best part of your life so far? How did it make you feel positive about yourself?

- Picture yourself as a confident person. Describe a typical day. How would you act or dress differently?

- What mistakes have you made in the past that prevent you from trying new things? What if you decided to 'try better' by using the wisdom you gained from those experiences?

- Why do you deserve to love yourself?

Using these prompts should help you start journaling the right way. Giving honest and truthful answers to them will set you on the path to building lasting healthy self-esteem. Journaling, if used properly, is a powerful tool for combating low self-worth. Remember, healthy self-esteem precedes a wholesome mind.

2. Meditation

And now for my next trick, I'll show you how to reprogram your mind without having brain surgery!

One powerful tool capable of producing seemingly magical results in building healthy self-esteem is meditation. Meditation is an act of keeping your mind fixed upon something for some time—it could be a thought, an activity, an incident, or a quote—to gain clarity. It is a form of deep reflection that relaxes the mind, rejuvenates the soul, and renews your mindset if done correctly.

Oftentimes, dealing with low self-esteem also means dealing intimately with negative thoughts, impostor syndrome, and feelings of inadequacy. This unwanted mental tango can weigh heavily on your mind and result in an overwhelming belief that you're not good enough. And we just can't have that. Because it's not true. This means you can't appreciate your unique skills and personality. Rather, your thinking is funneled through the lens of your self-defeating beliefs about yourself.

Battling low self-esteem will then mean dealing with the accompanying baggage that tries to rope you into believing you are not enough. It will mean replacing those negative thoughts about past deeds with positive ones, which is where meditation comes in. It is believed that to break a bad habit effectively, it must be replaced with a good one and done consistently. The same is true with building healthy self-esteem. Because the pattern of negative thoughts and imposter syndrome starts from the mind, building healthy self-esteem equally begins from the mind.

The best way to train the mind to be clearer, calmer, and more self-compassionate is through meditation. When we practice meditation for self-esteem, we learn that our criticisms and other negative thoughts are just thoughts. Not truths about ourselves. We can't stop negative thoughts, unfortunately. Forcing yourself to 'think positive' won't help either. Meditating reprograms your mind and attacks those negative thoughts at their source. Once your mind gets with the positive programming that meditation brings, it's much easier to see more positive than negative thoughts generated. Why, it's almost like magic, isn't it?

Look, I don't want to sound like a broken record. Mrs. Roberts, the friendly old lady who lives down the street, could go on and on about the same thing for hours. Bless her soul. While she's a sweet old lady, getting caught in conversation on the street with her gets tiring pretty quickly. I'll tell you about another magic trick I learned while spending time with Mrs. R. It's practically as good as meditation and twice as effective! Are you curious yet? I'll tell you in a bit!

Anyway, at the risk of pulling a Mrs. R on you, I just have to say that realizing the potential that lies in meditation is only the first step. I mean, it boosts your self-confidence and cancels out low self-esteem forever. That's a bold claim, but that's how certain I am about this. Understanding and accepting that the mind can be trained to produce an aura of self-confidence will liberate you from the fetters of low self-confidence into the freedom of healthy self-esteem.

Constantly engaging in meditation encourages a renewed outlook to self and life by extension.

How to Meditate

Effective meditation requires intentionality and constant practice. Make it a point of duty to practice the act of meditation every day. You can begin with a few minutes in a day and then increase the duration gradually. Because the human mind is prone to wandering, the first obstacle you must overcome is the need to be intentional but gentle with your mind. Also, because meditation requires full focus, there is a need to establish a no-distraction plan that will enable you to meditate effectively.

Below are steps that can aid effective meditation:

- Get a space free of distraction. As time goes on, you may not need this once you master the act of shutting out distraction. You'll be able to meditate in a low-noise environment.

- Set a timer. Five to ten minutes is perfect for a beginner.

- Make yourself comfortable and consciously focus on your breathing. Observe how you inhale and exhale.

- Choose what to meditate on and stay on course.

- Notice the state of your mind and quickly forgive your wandering thoughts.

- Rinse and repeat.

There you have it. Meditation takes a deliberate effort, and you get better with constant practice.

Mindfulness Meditation

This special type of meditation clears the mind by directing you to focus on the present moment. Being aware of the present helps you process your thoughts and drop the burden of negative thoughts.

It's a simple exercise that can be practiced anywhere and will take only five minutes. To practice mindfulness:

- Find a quiet space where you're not likely to be disturbed and get comfortable. You could either sit or lie down.

- Close your eyes and take a deep breath. Inhale deeply and slowly. Then exhale slowly. Keep doing this.

- Observe your breath. How does your chest and stomach move when you inhale and exhale?

- Focus on the simple action of breathing gently.

- Your mind, like a frisky puppy, is bound to wander. You could find yourself thinking about other things. Don't worry; just gently bring your mind back to your breath.

- Allow the thoughts and emotions you may feel float by without engaging them. Observe them, accept them, and let them go.

- Do this for five minutes.

- When your time is up, slowly open your eyes and leave when you feel ready to.

This exercise is famous for being misjudged because it seems so basic. I enjoy listening to people who had previously belittled the practice of mindfulness take back their words when they find out just how powerful the effects of mindfulness are. I look forward to hearing what you think when you try it out. Leave a comment on Amazon or shoot me an email. I live for this stuff!

Now, as we both know, practice makes perfect. A daily meditation practice can help you change your relationship with the thoughts and feelings that mess with your self-esteem. Do you want to build healthy self-esteem? Practice meditation and see how things begin to fall into place.

Things you can meditate on:

- **Lyrics of Music that reinforce your uniqueness as an individual.**

Music has been proven to have the capacity to connect with one's soul. Meditating on the lyrics of a powerful song broadens your mind. It cleanses your heart of negative thoughts and connects your soul to positivity, positively impacting your mind and promoting healthy self-esteem.

- **Quotes/books that reinforce your self-worth and confidence.**

Words are powerful and have the creative power of causing a complete change in mindsets. Choosing to meditate on good books opens you to the world of your true worth while silencing the lies you have accepted about yourself.

- **Conversations that highlight and appreciate your talents and uniqueness**

Conversations are made up of words. The words, in this case, are positive words spoken in love. Choosing to meditate on those words that highlight and appreciate your uniqueness has the magnitude to improve your self-worth and self-love. A good word spoken to you makes you happy and propels you to feel better about yourself. Meditating on good words spoken to you will further boost a healthy self-esteem.

- **Achievements that project your strength and skills.**

Meditating on your achievements helps you to see the unique prowess you possess. It helps you revel in your creative side, which reinforces your worth as an individual. This will eliminate any form of comparison or self-doubt.

There are other things you can meditate on, like your journey, work, relationship, a beautiful unforgettable incident, and so much more. In all, intentionally meditating on happy thoughts shifts your focus and mind from the negativity that permeates your mind. It gives you room to evaluate the important things in your life, open your heart to gratitude, and improve your self-confidence, self-worth, and self-esteem.

This sounds way too good to be true. There's gotta be a catch right?

Maybe something I'm not telling you? OK, you're right, you caught me.

Psych!

Sorry, couldn't resist. It really is as good as it sounds. Try it!

Benefits of Meditation.

Meditation has immense benefits that will have an overall impact on your mental health.

Below are some of the benefits of meditation for self-esteem:

- It helps break the pattern of negative thoughts.

- It improves self-awareness.

- It finds and boosts self-compassion.

- It helps build resilience.

- It directs you to focus on gratitude.

Meditation is a powerful self-care ritual tool capable of turning your self-esteem around for good.

3. Affirmations

Having healthy self-esteem simply means feeling good in your skin and recognising your worth. It means acknowledging and believing that you are a priceless gem and that your worth is inestimable. It is the understanding that you are unique as an individual and your life is not measured by your physical possessions. It also means your ability to forgive your past and not measuring your life on the pedestal of your past or your flaws.

Healthy self-esteem means accepting constructive criticism, being kind to yourself, and never comparing your life to others. It means having control over the negative thoughts that permeate your life. It means dwelling on your unique personality, making healthy choices, and taking responsibility for your actions.

You might be tempted to think maintaining healthy self-esteem is a lot of work, but it simply means knowing your worth and choosing to live in that reality daily. This doesn't exempt you from dealing with negative thoughts or self-doubt, but having healthy self-esteem helps you overcome this challenge. It helps you to stay in the reality of who you are unapologetically.

Affirmation is another effective self-care ritual that can boost healthy self-esteem. You may believe you are not good enough because a trusted significant figure in your life made careless statements about you in the past. You need to debunk these lies, and this is where affirmation comes in.

Affirmations help to replace negative thoughts with positive ones. They harness the mind's power by directing your intentions toward your best self and your happiest life. Also known as positive self-talk, they are known to lower stress levels in the body. The idea is to repeat the affirmations over and over while setting an intention for this affirmation. The goal is that if you repeat it often enough, you will believe the affirmation, and your behavior will change for the better.

The idea behind employing the use of affirmation to promote healthy self-esteem is that the words being repeatedly pronounced will find full expression in your subconscious mind, eventually translating to you accepting them as your true identity.

Affirmations are used to reaffirm your uniqueness, which improves self-love and self-acceptance. They don't hide your flaws or weaknesses; instead, they shift your attention from your flaws to your strengths. This alone is capable of bringing complete freedom from self-doubt and self-worthlessness.

You may think it's a waste of time and that repeating a few sentences won't change how you feel. But it's been scientifically proven that affirmations can rewire our thinking. This is because our brains can adapt to different circumstances, called "neuroplasticity." As a result, they can be tricked into confusing imagination with reality, and affirmations take advantage of this "loophole."

Research has shown that creating mental images of yourself in different situations with different abilities can trick your brain into thinking they're real. In addition, repeating positive affirmations leads to lower stress levels, improved quality of life, and feeling more comfortable in your skin (Kristenson, 2022).

There are hundreds of affirmations out there, and the best part is that you can create yours and stick with it if you need to. Just so you don't get overwhelmed, here are twenty great affirmations you can start with:

- I am loved and capable of being loved.

- My worth is not determined by other people's opinions.

- I am beautiful, intelligent, and unique.

- I am creative, strong, powerful, brave, and inspired.

- I deserve to feel good about myself.

- I can embrace my flaws and imperfections.

- I am honorable.

- I am worthy of good things.

- I am accepting myself unconditionally.

- I attract good things only.

- I am a good person who deserves to be treated with respect.

- My worth is inestimable.

- I am worthy of the compliments I receive.

- I am not afraid of the future.

- Fear does not rule my life.

- I make the right decisions and choices.

- Every day is another chance to shine.

- I am powerful with endless strength.

- My past does not define me.

- I am the best of my kind.

Consistently say these words loud, believe them, and watch the magic unfold. Remember that nobody can build your confidence for you. However, saying these magic words (move over Hogwarts!) will help you reconnect with your inner self and make you feel stronger. (Kristenson, 2022) I mean, you can see how affirmations are like magical spells right?

4. Gratitude

Gratitude means being thankful for something or someone. It also means the readiness to show appreciation for a kind or thoughtful deed extends to you. It precedes thanksgiving, and these two powerful tools help you appreciate your journey and consequently improve your self-esteem. Showing gratitude encourages you to become a deep thinker and a grateful soul. Gratitude isn't just about saying "Thank you." It is more of a revelation that opens your understanding to the little and big things that make you appreciate life and your journey as an individual. This explains why it is an effective self-care ritual for healthy self-esteem.

Gratitude is a thankful appreciation for what an individual receives, whether tangible or intangible. With gratitude, people acknowledge the goodness in their lives. In the process, people usually recognize the source of that goodness lies at least partially outside themselves. As a result, being grateful also helps people connect to something larger than themselves as individuals — whether to other people, nature, or a higher power.

This explains why showing gratitude for the air you breathe in and out sends a positive signal about you. It shows you know and appreciate the value of life. Showing gratitude for the weather reveals that you are cognizant of your environment, the beauty of nature, and the role it plays in making your life a better one. Showing gratitude for good health further reveals that you are mindful of how your spirit and soul connect with your body to enhance your sanity and total well-being. Appreciating the good people in your life projects you as someone who values people and the significant roles they play in your life. This promotes your happiness in your relationship.

In positive psychology research, gratitude is strongly and consistently associated with greater happiness. Gratitude helps people feel more positive emotions, relish good experiences, improve their health, deal with adversity, and build strong relationships.

How to show gratitude:

- Notice the little things you do not have to pay for (the air you breathe, the weather, sunshine, rain) and appreciate how they make your life better.

- Bring to mind a kind deed extended to you in the past, appreciate the person in your heart, put a call through, and send a gift or a thank you note to that person. This action empowers you to make others happy, which is the bedrock of healthy self-esteem.

- Consciously determine to appreciate your life and journey as an individual. Appreciate the lessons you have learned in life, how you get better every day, the good and bad choices you have made, and how you are consistently making progress. This act promotes self-appreciation leading to happier self-esteem.

Practicing the act of gratitude has a positive impact on your self-esteem. This act makes you feel alive, rejuvenated, and happy. If done consistently, it can change your mood and improve your temperament and relationship with other people. Gratitude also helps you to engage in mindful meditation, which improves your self-esteem and overall well-being.

5. Physical Exercise

Have you heard about the mind-body connection? A lot of people have tried to explain it in a lot of ways over the years. The basic principle here is that your mind and body are linked. Essentially, we can conclude that when we combine healthy physical practices with healthy mental practices, we're likely to achieve effective results.

Physical exercise is effective for restoring your self-esteem. Research has shown time and again that exercise can significantly increase our self-esteem. There are many mechanisms by which exercise increases our evaluations of ourselves. First, in the short-term, exercise enhances our mood and puts our minds in a more positive state. Second, in the long-term, exercise makes us feel good about our physical self – our abilities and physique. Last, and in both the short and long term, exercise provides us with a sense of accomplishment that boosts our confidence. Engaging in exercise as a self-care ritual can help promote healthy self-esteem.

Physical exercise is a proven mechanism that aids self-worth. It is a self-esteem-enhancing strategy that shifts your attention from negative thought patterns to positive ones. It helps you build tenacity and a can-do spirit. It helps you focus on your strength and appreciate your progress. Physical exercises give you a sense of healthy pride in yourself. It acts as a catalyst that propels you to do more and be a better person. In all, physical exercise catapults you from the zone of low self-esteem and doubt to a steady journey of healthy self-esteem. It helps reshape your negative mindset into a healthier one. The overall benefits of physical exercises are numerous; however, below are a few lists of these benefits:

- Improves your mental health

- Improves your brain function

- Reduces stress

- Improves your mood

- Gives you a sense of accomplishment

- Revamps your body and self-esteem

- Promotes self-love.

Following a regular exercise regime results in a remarkable improvement in self-worth and improves the overall quality of life. Below are some types of physical exercise that can help improve self-worth:

- Weight lifting exercises

- Aerobic Exercises (walking, jogging, running, swimming, biking)

- Yoga Postures (this is a two-in-one self-care routine. Yoga allows you to combine meditation with physical exercise.)

- Cardio Exercises (Burpees, long jump, squat jump, jumping jack, etc.)

Engaging in constant physical exercises is a form of self-care. It shows that you love yourself enough to care about your physical and mental health. It reveals that you are taking deliberate actions to keep fit, making you feel so good about yourself. It shows that you understand that building healthy self-esteem is an intentional journey you embark on.

So we can agree that nothing says 'I love myself' more than a good 20-minute workout session. Awesome. But let's be real; it's entirely possible to have times where you lag behind with being physically fit. That's fine. You need to be kind to yourself whenever this happens. If you don't feel motivated to keep up with your exercises, your affirmations can swoop in and drop off some fresh motivation!

After all, you are on a journey to building healthy self-esteem, and sometimes the road to our destinations is bumpy and rough. Do not be too hard on yourself. Get up, keep fit, and improve your overall health and self-esteem.

6. Getting Support from Support Groups

Support groups can lend you a solid shoulder to lean on. Such communities provide shelter from your insecurities because you have a sense of belonging and the knowledge that you are never alone in your struggles. You find people of like minds with a unified struggle in such communities.

Mental health support groups can help you improve your self-esteem. They help because sometimes, we need to build self-esteem and an increased connection with others. For people living with low self-esteem, it can sometimes feel like you're the only one struggling with this problem. But the reality is that many people also live with low self-esteem, whether that's because of a mental health condition or as a standalone issue. (Woolfe,2019).

When you join a new support group, you may be nervous about sharing personal issues with people you don't know. At first, you may benefit from simply listening. Over time, however, contributing your own ideas and experiences may help you get more out of a support group. Try a support group for a few weeks. If it doesn't feel like a good fit for you, consider a different support group or a different support group format.

In this case, considering a different support group format may mean having a trusted buddy who can help you unburden your worries, gradually ease you into exploring the support group option, and accept to be a member of such a community if you find it hard to identify with one.

Have you ever heard that you start to become like the five people you spend the most time with? It is so important that you surround yourself with positive people, with friends who will give you an honest but positive assessment of who you are and your worth. If you find that the folks you are hanging around send you into a negative spiral, it might be time to find a new tribe. This new tribe must consist of a trusted buddy. Because one of the ways to gradually build healthy self-esteem is to have a trusted buddy in your circle. Your trusted buddy will be your accountability partner, and vice versa. Nonetheless, be careful your buddy is someone on the same page as you.

Avoid people who are good at battering your self-esteem. Engaging them or keeping them around you will frustrate your effort to build healthy self-esteem. Keeping them in your close circle will bring you to ground zero and make it more difficult to achieve your purpose. So, this is why it's important to hang out with someone on the same page as you with your best interests at heart. It does not have to be someone within your friends and family circle but someone with whom you can be vulnerable.

Finding a support group in your locality or even creating one greatly benefits your self-esteem. One important benefit of having a trusted buddy or being a member of a support group is that you have the chance to practice self-care rituals (journaling, affirmation, gratitude, physical exercise) together. Practicing these self-care rituals together keeps you in check and accountable. It allows you to check up on each other, measure your progress, and encourage each other, which will boost your self-esteem. Practicing these self-care rituals with your group members opens your eyes and mind to deeper levels of understanding the dynamics of how to build and maintain healthy self-esteem. In all, a support group is mutually beneficial to achieving your goals.

When you're struggling, sometimes it's best to seek insight from others who know what you're going through. In a support group, you may meet people much older than you who have lived with low self-esteem for years and have found ways of coping. They might be able to share experiences on their triggers, how they have tried to build self-esteem over the years, and what they currently do to feel valuable and confident amid depression. In a support group for low self-esteem, people can talk about all sorts of things that have helped them to build self-esteem, including books, articles, podcasts, therapies, workshops, courses, hobbies, and lifestyle changes. (Woolfe 2019)

Constantly engaging and communicating with support groups helps you to redefine your self-worth. This also promotes self-love because you belong to a community of reliable friends who see, know, and accept you for who you are. This is why having a great and reliable support system promotes self-awareness and self-love.

Benefits of a support group:

1. It provides a safe haven to unburden and get encouragement

A support group provides you with a safe place to unburden and allay your fears and insecurities. It is a judgment-free zone that encourages you to be vulnerable without fear of being exposed. Since you are all working towards a common goal, you are not ashamed to be vulnerable with this group of people.

2. It helps you identify with people with the same struggle

Signing up to be a support group member allows you to relate with people with the same struggle. You get to meet people from all walks of life and benefit from their wealth of knowledge and experiences.

3. It helps you gain a sense of empowerment, control, or hope.

Interacting with people with similar struggles gives you a sense of empowerment. It gives you a sense of renewed hope and control. This group of people helps amplify your strength without being judgmental. You gain a deeper perspective of the real you through these people, which helps you feel more in control of your life. These benefits help you review and renew your desire to be a better version of yourself daily. They propel you never to give up on building unshakeable healthy self-esteem.

4. It helps improve your skills to cope with challenges

Your interaction with the support group members exposes you to various challenges peculiar to low self-esteem and how individuals have been able to overcome them. This helps improve your skills to cope with the same challenge.

5. It promotes your interpersonal relationship

One of the traits of low self-esteem is shyness. You are critical of yourself and mostly unwilling to relate with other people. Being an active support group member helps you learn how to interact with people. It also promotes a sense of communal acceptance. In fact, you can use this group to practice how to maintain eye contact and public speaking. An individual with healthy self-esteem is confident to express him/herself with no fear of being judged. Thus, a support group aids self-confidence and healthy self-esteem.

The benefits attached to a support group are enormous when it comes to building healthy self-esteem. However, it is recommended that you take your time to find and identify with a support group that aligns with your goal of building healthy self-esteem. It is okay to watch and determine if the group will meet your needs. It is also okay to decline to join a support group that does not align with your goal. In all, find a reliable support system you are comfortable with and give yourself the chance and patience to evolve.

Self-Care Worksheet

Self-Care Checkup

Self-care is important, but for any self-care plan worth its salt, you should know that self-compassion is an invaluable part of it.

We can improve our well-being and preserve excellent mental health by engaging in self-care activities.

These can include ingrained, everyday behaviors like healthy eating and regular exercise, which frequently fall by the wayside during particularly trying or stressful times in our lives.

Understanding how frequently or well we engage in self-care activities can help us spot areas where we are falling short and make improvements for greater mental health.

Instructions

You can use this Self-Care Checkup to evaluate how frequently and effectively you practice self-care in five key areas of your life:

1. Emotional

2. Physical

3. Social

4. Professional, and

5. Spiritual self-care.

Rate how well or frequently you think you engage in each activity by using the key provided below. You should note that the list is not exhaustive. This means that while you might find some unappealing, you might also want to include some activities. You can go right ahead and add your own ideas.

Emotional self-care

Activities	The rate at which you engage in them (1-10)
Enjoying your hobbies	
Taking a break from technology/social media	
Appreciating your talents, strengths, and accomplishments	
Learning/exploring new things	
Taking a vacation or mini break	
Being at ease and laughing about things	
Expressing your emotions and feelings through talking, journaling, etc.	

Taking a break from responsibilities	
Engaging in self-nurturing activities like a day at the spa, a warm bath, etc.	
General emotional self-care	

Physical self-care

Activities	The rate at which you engage in them (1-10)
Regular health checkups	
Drinking enough water	
Eating healthily	
Resting when unwell	
Eating regularly	

Drinking enough water	
Exercising regularly/keeping fit	
Maintaining a good hygiene	
General physical self-care	

Social self-care

Activities	The rate at which you engage in them (1-10)
Quality time with friends and family	
Keeping contact with distant connections through social media or skype	
Quality time with partner	
Making new friends or connecting with new people	

Having mentally stimulating discussions	
Engaging in fun group activities	
Honoring invitations	
Outings with friends	
Overall social self-care	

Professional self-care

Activities	The rate at which you engage in them (1-10)
Asking for help at work when necessary	
Maintaining a positive work environment	
Socializing with coworkers	

Taking lunch breaks and other work breaks	
Having a great work-life balance	
Turning down unreasonable tasks	
Accepting new/interesting tasks or projects	
Pursuing development opportunities in your career	
Seeking recognition/reward/promotion where deserved	
General professional self-care	

Spiritual self-care

Activities	The rate at which you engage in them (1-10)
Staying outdoors or enjoying nature walks	
Volunteering	
Meditation	
Practicing gratitude	
Involved in religion	
Having alone time to self-reflect	
Applying your strengths, values, or talents	
Appreciating art, music, literature, etc.	
Practicing general spiritual self-care	

CHAPTER 8

Releasing Your History: Forgiving Those Who Hurt You

"I think the first step is to understand that forgiveness does not exonerate the perpetrator. Forgiveness liberates the victim. It's a gift you give yourself."

- T.D Jakes

A Background on Forgiveness

It doesn't matter whether Momma taught you *better than that* when it comes to staying mad at someone. All those lessons can be moot points in the face of serious hurt and betrayal, especially when it comes from someone who was supposed to have your back. If we were taught to forgive others when they hurt us, the question is why is it still so damn hard now that we're adults?

In reality, unforgiveness is the following things in disguise:

1. Fear of getting hurt again

2. Hatred for exploitation

3. Desire to punish

Humans are hardwired to avoid pain. So it adds up to avoid the pain of getting hurt, which can be a lot. We tend to remember what wrong was done to us because that memory can help us avoid getting into the same situation in future. It's a protective instinct, at least when we view it from a natural standpoint. To avoid getting exploited again, our brain registers the pain, and that's when we also find it hard to let it go.

In light of that, we can say that forgiveness deviates from what's natural. It's far from what we'd do— what we're wired to do. It's the exact opposite.

Perspective 1: Forgiveness is for you, not for them

Karen stayed mad at her dad for years because he abandoned them (her mother and siblings). Unfortunately, he passed away before Karen could reconcile with him. She has since carried the weight of resentment and guilt about how everything turned out. On several occasions before he died, her father reached out to her to make peace, but she was adamant. She said she wanted him to have a taste of his own medicine. In the long run, getting her pound of flesh turned out to be way more expensive than she thought.

I eventually met Karen when she had arrived at her wits' end, tired of the anger issues that kept her losing precious relationships and opportunities. One of our earliest sessions was spent reviewing what she had lost on account of her deep-seated anger. Maybe Karen's burden would have been lessened if she had given room for forgiveness. And on time too. Sadly, she still had to do it even after her father was already six feet below the ground.

Did that last part strike you, or was it just me?

If we still have to forgive a dead person to find peace, isn't it clear that forgiveness is not for the other person but for us?

I'll say this, but I promise it's just gonna be this one time: Pretty clear, Captain!

Perspective 2: If revenge is sweet, why does it leave such a bitter taste?

A name is coming to me. That's right. John Wick. Great movie. Love, passion, war, and unforgiveness. The classic ingredients that make up the recipe for disaster. John went from frying pan to fire in his quest for revenge. Maybe it was all worth it for him, but it definitely took everything away. Eh.

Speaking mildly now, we tend to forget the sweet memories we once created with current offenders, that's assuming the offender is a loved one or close folk. Who'd blame us? I get it; the gravity of offense varies. Expecting you to forgive someone who stood you up or accused you wrongly is a little bit hard. But what about bringing to mind how we have also wrongly accused someone or tarnished someone's image (even if it was not intentional) in the past? It's a valid consideration to weigh.

Your offender may also be oblivious to the extent to which you are offended or how much they have hurt you, so why not let them out of there? Not so fast, I know; it is never easy to forgive or forget, but I do know it is easier to choose to forgive. By choosing to forgive, you rid your mind of toxicity while permitting yourself to heal.

There are two other things we can do instead of forgiving:

1. Get revenge

2. Just stay angry

Believe me, both look like more juicier options than forgiving, but they're not. Getting revenge is plain stressful. Gosh, you have to make a plan and everything. Staying angry will hurt the muscles of your dear heart.

But forgiveness?

It'll free you. It'll liberate you; you'll breathe! You'll feel good. In fact, your offender might be worse off because if they expect to see you sulk and hurt, you'll disarm them by being so free.

In the spirit of self-compassion and self-love, you need to grab whatever can release you from unnecessary pain and difficulty with both hands. Unforgiveness is a cage you put yourself in that squeezes peace out of you daily. You gotta let go.

Perspective 3: To err is human.

Understanding that to err is human means the human species (which includes me and you) is prone to err. And this means you and I are not exempted from erring, even when we err on the side of caution. Understanding this will help us to examine ourselves before casting a stone. The point I am trying to make is that by choosing to forgive, you'll be letting go of so much baggage and through a simple understanding that sometimes, we all need forgiveness.

Perspective 4: Forgiving a person doesn't mean they have changed.

I, however, need you to understand that choosing to forgive does not exonerate the perpetrator nor does it right the wrong that has been done. It also doesn't mean they have changed or are now magically a new person. It doesn't even mean they're sorry for what they did to you. It simply means you have chosen to heal and overlook their wrongdoings while creating and establishing a healthy boundary. Healthy boundaries provide a good stimulant to your self-esteem and help protect you from getting hurt again in the same way.

How Is Forgiveness Tied to Self-esteem?

Healthy self-esteem comprises the ability to forgive yourself of your past and not measure your life on the pedestal of your past or your flaws. Can you see a correlation between these two? It is, therefore, safe to affirm that forgiveness is one of the pathways to healthy self-esteem. If we go by the definition above, we will realize that at different points in life, we all need to extend our power of forgiveness to ourselves. While we're at it, we can also extend compassion to that friend, colleague, sibling, or whoever the offender is.

Don't forget that choosing to forgive is a choice you have made that will have an overall effect on your self-esteem. This choice further reveals that you understand there are limitations to human abilities, and you choose to walk in that reality. Tell me if this will not have a ripple effect on your self-esteem. The answer to this is in the affirmative. Yes!!! Choosing to forgive shows that you love yourself enough to rid your mind and heart of the hurt, resentment, and anger caused by the unjust treatment meted out to you. It means your heart and mind are now free to accommodate positive thoughts and vibes, producing a blast of fresh air to your self-esteem.

The Crucial Importance of Letting Go

When you let go, you experience an overwhelming feeling of liberation.

If you succumb to the natural reaction of wanting to punish the offender or giving the silent treatment, the joke will be on you. You'll get hurt more by carrying the weight and burden. But by letting go, you'll set yourself free from that weight's shackles. Forgiveness gives you the liberty to thrive and move ahead. I understand it is a difficult thing to do. Letting go may seem like you are being stripped of your power to avenge yourself. But believe me, you will set yourself free from much more hurt. Forgiveness is a gift you give yourself.

One other reason why letting go is crucially important is that by forgiving, you'll be breaking a vicious cycle and choosing to pass on kindness instead. Do you know each time you bring to mind the wrongdoing or unjust treatment meted out to you, you tend to hate more, look for suitable retribution, and literally wish the offender multiple times evil? But does this lessen the pain? Your guess is as good as mine. Instead, it aggravates the pain; let that go on long enough, and you may have to deal with emotional issues you didn't sign up for.

To further explain the importance of letting go, take the example of your relationship with your spouse or a loved one. Over time, these relationships are actually a combination of joy, hurt, and forgiveness. Can you bring to mind any unpleasant incident between y'all? How you stayed mad for a while, how you tried to avoid them and how your heart beat faster each time you were in close proximity to them. Did you feel better when you finally made up with each other? Was it like, phew, now we can go back to enjoying that game together? Exactly my point. Forgiveness is indispensable in moving your relationship forward.

This is equally applicable to you. Forgiveness is important to move you forward. Harboring the hurt, guilt, and pain makes you static. It leaves you stuck at one particular point as far as that side is concerned, and only forgiveness gives you the liberty to move ahead. Choosing to forgive succinctly means you are writing a new story of freedom. And that in itself opens you to a new world of possibilities and hope. No kidding.

To wrap up on the importance of letting go, let's do a quick summary.

- It liberates you.

- It moves you and your relationship forward.

- It breaks the vicious cycle of hurt.

- It is a gift you give yourself

- It is your way of writing a new story of freedom.

There you have it; each time you are tempted to stay in the zone of unforgiveness, do me a favor, bring these points to mind, and move forward.

Should You Forgive and also Forget?

Yes, you should forgive, but you may never be able to forget because our minds are made up of experiences (past, present, the good, the bad, and the ugly). Plus, our lives are made up of memories (both pleasant and unpleasant) and forgetting them means denying a part of our history.

Everyone has experienced a measure of injustice in their lives. Some of these injustices are so grave that it will take several years to find forgiveness. And even when you get to the point of letting it all go, there will always be reminders. Even when time heals those painful experiences, they are the events that make up our memories. This explains why forgiveness does not automatically mean you will forget.

A person who went through sexual abuse will inevitably live with that memory for the rest of her life. The same applies to someone who was bullied a lot in high school. These victims might forgive the offenders, but they cannot deny those experiences because it is part of their history. They may choose to forgive and move on, but the truth is those experiences shaped them and their outlook on life. I am sure you can relate to this.

Forgiving can be hard, but it's possible while forgetting is almost if not impossible. This is because your mind housed the painful betrayal you experienced and also helped you process the pain. Once your mind has gone through this process, it'll remind you of the pain you have gone through to prevent a recurrence. Your brain will remind you that once beaten, twice shy. It will remind you of the phrase, "fool me once, shame on you; fool me twice, shame on me." In a bid to protect you from a recurrence, you'll get reminded of the past wrongdoing or unjust treatment meted out to you, and you'll become defensive in order not to be hurt for the second time. Here, your mind acts as a protective shield.

Forgiveness is a choice you make to abandon willfully (not forget) resentment and related responses. This translates to you taking deliberate actions to suspend but not forget the pain that comes with that wrongdoing. Again, I affirm that you can forgive but may be unable to forget because the neurons in your brain are wired to house memories (either good or bad).

How to Let Go of Those Who Hurt You

So far, we have established that offenses are part of the human relationship. I understand that letting go is hard but remember, we have talked about the importance of letting go. To further help you on this journey of forgiveness, let us find the antidotes to those hurts you feel. Below are a few ways to help you forgive and let go of those who hurt you:

- **Remember What Forgiveness Entails**

You are not excusing or denying that the wrong act happened; you are only choosing to let go because you know that you deserve that peace of mind. Once you realize over and over again that forgiveness is yours to give, it becomes easy for you to let go of the offender.

- **Talk About It**

Because you have been hurt, it is important you let it out in any format suitable for you. You can talk about this in your journal or to a friend or even meditate on it. Talking about it also means permitting yourself to shed some tears if necessary. And this gives you the space and pace to heal. You will equally discover that talking about it helps lessen the pain. It can be very therapeutic. It can also double as a catalyst that propels you to let go completely.

- **Determine and Choose to Let Go Each Time Your Mind Wanders to that Experience.**

We've talked about how it's hard to forget what wrong someone did to you completely. So it's very likely that once in a while, even after forgiving, you might remember again and then again. To help you truly forgive the offender, choose always to let go when you are reminded of those bad experiences. When you practice this over time, you will realize that your spirit, soul, and body will gradually align with this.

- **Be Empathetic, Considerate, and Reasonable**

Sometimes, the other person didn't mean to hurt you and might already be feeling terrible for what they did. Some empathy from you will help move things along in the right direction. Being empathetic means putting yourself in the offender's shoes. Flip the coin and truthfully examine if you can do that same thing yourself. We sometimes need someone to give us a bit of compassion too. This realisation will help you understand that to err is indeed human, but you can choose to forgive. Choosing to forgive projects you as a considerate and reasonable being, which can help you forgive many times.

On a final note, I would like to say that because human relationship is delicate, choosing to forgive promotes your relationship with a contrite offender. Forgiveness can help you bond more deeply with the erring party as long as they're truly sorry for hurting you.

Forgiving those who hurt you and living free of the pain that comes with staying mad will help free up space in your heart so you can focus on much-needed self-love. Besides, what's self-love when you're still hating someone? It'll be like constantly undoing your own efforts. And we don't want that.

Practicing Forgiveness Workbook for You

It's not easy to forgive, yes. Letting go of all that hurt, all that pain won't come easy. But forgiving someone doesn't mean denying their wrongdoing, condoning, or excusing them. Forgiveness involves letting go of all anger and negative feelings associated with the person and situation.

To practice this forgiveness exercise, it's not a must that you confront the person directly. The exercise involves indirectly confronting those who hurt you by writing it out:

1. Create a forgiveness list: write out the names of everyone you feel has hurt you and you're finding it hard to let go. Dead or alive, anyone can make it to your list.

_____

_____

_____

_____

_____

_____

2. First, pick a person on your list and write down everything you feel this person has done to wrong you.

_____

_____

_____

_____

_____

_____

3. Practice telling that person everything you want them to know about how they hurt you. Be confident and specific; let it all out.

_____

_____

_____

_____

_____

4. Write down the positive thing(s) this person might have done for you. It's okay if you can't think of or remember any.

_____

_____

_____

_____

_____

_____

5. Practice telling them you forgive them because they didn't know any better.

_____

_____

_____

_____

_____

_____

After this is done, practice this exercise for every other person on your list until you're done. You're going to feel lighter with all the weight of the pain and hurt gone once you're done with this exercise.

CHAPTER 9

End People-Pleasing

There is a syndrome that makes people with low self-esteem push themselves to be overly kind and generous to just about everyone. Mostly, they are so cautious in their actions and reactions because they don't want to be in anyone's wrong book. They will go to any length to do just about anything to get good appraisals from everyone they meet. They feel bad and downcast when anyone says anything negative about them.

In the real sense, there is nothing wrong with your acts of generosity and demonstration of kindness at every given opportunity. I know no better way to make our world better than such acts of love. However, those times when you had to make other people happy at the expense of your happiness indicate you have this syndrome commonly found in people with low self-esteem. Wait, wait, you'll soon find out what this syndrome is.

There are similar instances of such indications like giving up your seat to someone else to get close to them or opting for food you don't like because everyone in your group chose it, or ditching your favorite color of cloth to choose one that your friend chose because you don't want to look different from your friend, etc.

Come to think of this, is there any rule that says you shouldn't be happy while making others happy?

Don't you think that the stranger you are trying to get close to has other alternatives for getting a seat without taking yours?

Didn't each person in the group you joined pay for the food they get to eat, including you? Why should the group, or anyone else, decide what you choose to eat when they did not pay for it?

Did your friend choose to be your friend because you have similar color preferences? Why should that count now in your friendship?

It's okay if you are trying to make the world a better place for everyone around you. But you also have to be a better version of yourself to enjoy the better place you create for everyone else; everyone will enjoy the world you created for them while you are either hiding somewhere, hurting and recuperating from the wounds you incurred.

Newsflash: You're not a martyr.

Doing things at the expense of your self-esteem is bad. This kind of act makes you tilt from being generous to becoming a people-pleaser.

Yes, people-pleasing is the syndrome evident in people with low self-esteem.

How People-Pleasing Works

Erika Myers, a therapist in Bend, Oregon, described people-pleasing as changing your words or behaviors to suit another person's reactions. This is synonymous with the character of a particular animal, a chameleon. A chameleon does this as a way to survive any perceived threat.

It is a Desire to Fit in: For someone who tries to bend in different situations, theirs might not be because they perceive any threat but they just want to be accepted. They want to fit in. They want the validation of other people, so they bend to the will of others.

Think of a teenager like Shirley, who has a natural talent to sing – a great gift that could land her a spot at the America's Got Talent audition. But here is Shirley; no one really knows her except her immediate family and a few friends. Then there is Vanessa, who attends the same school as Shirley. The students love Vanessa because she sings the kind of songs they want to hear. They chant her name and adore her. From a distance, she seems to have everything going well; she has a great background and is famous.

Shirley feels intimidated (perceived threat) whenever she sees Vanessa. She feels threatened by her presence. To eliminate this threat, Shirley starts doing just about anything Vanessa likes to do, from the clothes she prefers to the genre of songs and to the places she goes. She upgrades her lifestyle to get noticed like Vanessa. She lies about her parentage to get people's approval.

According to Erika Myers, Shirley's predicament damages herself and her relationships.

Shirley can never realize her worth so long as she keeps striving to please people by trying to become like someone else.

It is an inward perception: The truth about people-pleasing is that it's first an inward perception before an outward demonstration. While the outward demonstration of kindness can make people applaud you and feel drawn to you, your inward perception of such demonstration can be wrong.

If you try to do good to everyone around you because you want to appear good to them and no one will think bad about you, your perception is wrong and damaging because it's impossible to be good to everyone.

It is sometimes a Quest to be the Good Sheep of the Family: You have food preferences, right? Must you love everything your parents prepare? But then, you try to eat just everything every time because you want to make your parents happy with you. That is one illustration of people-pleasing within a family setting.

Has your older sibling ever asked you to help them with their homework while they go out with a couple of friends when you have piles of homework to do yourself? If you jump on the task every time they ask because you don't want your older sibling to think anything negative about you, you are a people-pleaser. You'll deny yourself of good sleep because you'll have to stay up late into the night to complete both homework? That's not cool.

Symptoms of People-Pleasing Tendencies in You

At this point, you should have begun to know whether you are a people-pleaser. But to clear all doubts, the following are signs you can look out for to know if you are a people-pleaser or identify one when you see them.

1. You are a Yes-Yes Person

Are there people who don't know how to say "No" to people? Yes! There are quite a number of them. They feel if they say no, they might offend the other person. Just because they don't want to be the reason for anyone's sad look, they say yes to them, even if it's inconvenient.

2. Passivity

Another symptom is that people in this category try to avoid taking any action or saying anything at all to avoid conflict. Sometimes just saying "yes" can create some conflicts, especially when you are in a situation where two people demand differing responses from you. So you say nothing because you don't want to take sides, and you don't want to offend either party.

Inwardly, you know it feels wrong, but you choose to be indifferent because, in your view, it's safer that way.

3. Always Seeking a Thumbs-Up

People in this category always want to get people's approval. When they are asked to give a speech, they try as much as they can to say things that will arouse their listeners, even if it feels wrong. When asked to put up a performance, they put a lot of energy into acting with the sole objective of getting their director's approval. They don't like to get negative criticism. Their perception of negative criticism is that it means they have failed. Therefore, they work hard to please everyone watching them.

Anytime negative criticisms are doled out to them, they immediately withdraw into their shells for a long duration. They feel dejected. It's like they have been dealt a significant blow. It will be hard for them ever to try anything like that again.

4. You Always Sacrifice Your Happiness for Others

This is a silent way of depriving yourself of the good things in life. When people go out of their way to make others happy while they suffer for it, they may be overly trying to please people.

They smile while hurting so long the person they are trying to please is happy and safe. But afterward, they retire to a solitary place to be alone and to nurse their wounds.

Does that sound weird? But it happens!

5. You Always Take the Blame for Everything

People-pleasers feel it's just right to take the blame for every conflict or misunderstanding. They do this because they don't want the other person to be seen as bad. They defend the character of the other party while theirs get smeared.

6. They Mistake Dehumanization for Being Humane

Some people might think it's humane to get hurt for others to be happy. For some, they were raised to believe so; it's part of their custom. While they think they are doing humanity some good, they are actually depriving themselves of enjoying the benefits of being human themselves.

How People-Pleasing Affects Self-Esteem

The most devastating damage people-pleasing does to you doesn't tell on your body but on your inner being. I'll tell you what gets affected when you toll the path of people-pleasing:

1. Loss of Identity

By the time Shirley, from my first illustration in this chapter, tries to fit into every character like Vanessa's, she would have become Vanessa, the famous girl in school, while the real Shirley will be lost somewhere in the seas.

To try to please people is to risk the chances of losing who you are – your identity. The only thing that will be visible is the personality the people have created. So your body will be carrying a dead "You" within and carrying the people's identity simultaneously. Just imagine how heavy that could be. The weight of that can sink you into depression and self-resentment.

Tell me, how long can you carry a dead and fake identity together in your frail body?

2. Loss of Personal Values

In trying to please people, you'll lose your personal values because you'll have to jettison them to bend to the people's values if you want to please them. What are you without your personal values? In the long run, you'll become a puppet who dances to every tune.

Oh, I need to warn you beforehand that a lot of people can be bad puppeteers. There is no pleasing them in the real sense. They will use you till they achieve their own ends. You'll always be at their bidding.

Do you still think of a personal value in such a context? It no longer exists. Even though they reward you with what they call privileged-friendship or some other meager benefits, they will rob you of the things you stand for.

3. Loss of Creativity

This effect might not be immediate, but when you begin to see it, you should know that you have wandered too far in the maze of people-pleasing.

People-pleasing makes you doubt your abilities; it makes you feel others are better than you, so you have to do the things they do the way they do them, and in the process, you lose your individuality and creativity.

Do you think it's really worth it?

4. Loss of Voice

In the process of trying to please others, you lose your own voice. Nothing you say really matters; you rather accept other people's opinions than air your own view. Even if your whole being refused other people's opinions, you take in theirs because you don't want to offend them, or if it's in a group, you don't want to dance against the current.

The result is that you secretly resent yourself for doing what others decide, and you hate yourself for not, at least, saying what you think about the whole issue.

If you don't do something about it, gradually, you'll begin to accept your place as a second class whose voice doesn't matter.

Hey! Is that what you really want for yourself?

How to Put a Stop to People-Pleasing

Is it even possible to stop something that has grown in your subconscious mind? Yes, it is! Now, if you approach this aspect with a passive mindset, you'll not get any results.

You have to be tired of getting burnt every time you try to salvage your relationship, help your older brother, or get close to a student in your school to stop this act.

Also, I'll tell you beforehand that the result won't come at once, but you must make up your mind not to give up midway. Let us see this through together by following these steps:

Step 1: Stop Hanging Your Head Down

The first thing you must do is raise your head high and believe in yourself. You cannot recover your self-worth by always looking down on yourself. Hanging your head down is a sign of defeat and doubt.

Stop being so glum!

For so long, you have allowed yourself to dance to the tune of others. Now, I will allow you to dance to one more tune. I am chanting a new melody to you, and it's a tune that permits you to raise your head high.

Step 2: Redefine Your Values

This is a very important step. You must redefine what you stand for and want to be known for. You have to stop being an "everybody" person. Everybody has their own values except you. That, too, must change from this moment.

Redefine your value system and decide to let them influence your actions and relationship with people.

Step 3: Put Yourself First

Who deserves to be happy first, if not you? Who deserves me-time more than anyone else? Who deserves to get time off after completing their task?

Yes, you do!

Learn to put yourself first. You cannot genuinely love others if you don't love yourself first; that is the golden rule.

Step 4: Resign from Being a Yes-Yes person

This is one tough decision you must make, but you have to make it anyway. Resolve to say No to any task, request, or invitation inconvenient for you.

Resolve not to take in just about everything that comes your way. Set boundaries to what you can take or do, where you can go or visit. Let this choice be based on your personal convictions, not on the interest of any other person.

Saying No won't make you a bad person; it will only make you a person with a will of their own.

Step 5: Speak Up!

Stop cowering or shying away from giving your opinion about things. Your voice counts. Let nothing tell you otherwise. If your opinion counts, then let it be heard loudly.

Ending People Pleasing Worksheet

If pleasing people is your long-term habit, putting an end to it will be pretty difficult. The more you please people at the detriment of your own needs, the more your resentment builds up. To stop people-pleasing, you have to go from lying and pretending to yourself and start telling yourself the truth. This exercise will help you achieve that.

1. Recall some instances when you practiced people-pleasing. What reasons or excuses did you give for not saying no to your detriment?

_____

_____

_____

_____

_____

_____

_____

_____

2. Do you agree that you could have said no in these instances?

_____

_____

_____

_____

_____

_____

_____

_____

3. If the situation came up again, would you actually say no?

_____

_____

_____

_____

_____

_____

_____

4. What do you honestly want for yourself?

_____

_____

_____

_____

_____

_____

_____

5. How will you stay strong in future scenarios to avoid going back to your default setting of people-pleasing?

_____

_____

_____

_____

_____

_____

_____

6. Are you ready to feel uncomfortable and tell people the truth no matter what?

_____

_____

_____

_____

_____

_____

7. When it gets uncomfortable, will you smooth things over by people-pleasing or stick to your commitment?

_____

_____

_____

_____

_____

_____

_____

8. Why do you think you find it easier to give in and agree?

_____

_____

_____

_____

_____

_____

9. Why do you think you're uncomfortable with disagreeing with people?

_____

_____

_____

_____

_____

_____

_____

10. What's the worst that could happen if you disagree?

_____

_____

_____

_____

_____

_____

Chapter 10

Ending Self-esteem Battering Relationships and Building Healthy Ones

I've shown you things you need to do to redeem your self-worth, love yourself without apology, and live your life to the fullest. Those are parts of the few steps you need to take leading up to your reinvention and unleashing your inner beauty. Return to the previous chapters to practice everything I suggested as it applies to your context to get the result we envisaged.

You need to do a few more things for this practical approach to recovering your self-esteem to be holistic. Here, we'll assess the impact of your relationships on your self-esteem.

A lot of us are mostly influenced by the circle of friends we walk with. And some characters we exhibit are most times traceable to the company we keep.

Think of the time you just resumed high school. Do you remember how naïve and reserved you were? But after a few days in school, you began to mingle with a few students with whom you felt you had something in common. Then the bond began to grow from just being colleagues;

you became friends that must see each other every day in school, go to the cafeteria together, share a bunch of gists and laugh over them together, etc.; it was all fun for you.

But did you realize that as the bond grew, you began to take on your friends' vocab and talk like them and react to things like them? This is a natural fact that relationships' impact on your personality can influence what you think about yourself and the values you adopt.

Relationships are supposed to be enjoyed, but when one party begins to suffer in the relationship and they are no longer having fun, as it were, in the relationship, that relationship is no longer healthy, and it can have negative impacts on your mental health – affecting aspects of your core being.

If you have had one of such bad experiences, you'll understand what it means to be in a toxic relationship. But do you think avoiding relationships totally and shutting your heart to people is the best way to go? You could be hurting yourself even more if you choose to isolate yourself. That was why I spoke about forgiving yourself in one of the previous chapters. You should revisit it.

You cannot survive in isolation. We were all born to live with other people and live in a community. However, when any relationship within a community begins to deprive you of the happiness, love, and fulfillment you are entitled to in the community, you have the right to cut off that relationship because it's cancerous. You don't have to cut off everybody from your life, just the cancerous ones.

How to Identify Relationships That Are Affecting Your Self-Esteem

To be clear on the term "relationships," it's not limited to relationships between boys and girls; it transcends it. It covers relationships between same-sex friends as well. As a girl, you have relationships with other girls in your school, community, or places of worship. The same thing goes for boys too. Any of these forms of relationship that batters your personality is not good for you.

Here are a few signs to help you identify such relationships:

#1 Your Presence is not Acknowledged

Any relationship you are in that doesn't acknowledge your presence points to the fact that you are not so relevant after all. In a case like this, your friends or parents ignore you as though you don't really matter. Even if you are in the same room with them, they ignore you like you are not really there.

Whatever might be their reason for doing that, it's doing you no good. Who doesn't like to be recognized, especially among people you consider to be your close circle? Statements such as, "Oh, I didn't realize you're here," and "Did you say something just now." (this is after saying a lot of things to your friend who was obviously not listening to you)

If this repeats itself several times, you'll begin to feel insignificant. This is not good for your self-esteem.

#2 Your Opinions are Dismissed

Friend: "What do you think about this?"

You: "Taking a music major will be good for your musical career."

Friend: "Never mind. My uncle knows better."

If every time your friend asks you for your opinion, they end up dismissing whatever you say. you'll begin to feel reluctant to want to say anything another time. That can damage your confidence to speak up any other time.

#3 You are Always Silenced

A closer signal to being dismissed is when you are not allowed to speak at all. Just when you are about to talk, your friend or parent chimes in, "I know what he wants …" or "She would not mind if you take her out for dinner." And because you don't want to embarrass yourself or your friend or parent, you just respond with a smile to show your consent.

That is dangerous for your mental health because whoever is doing that to you is taking away your voice and your power to make the right choice for yourself.

It might sound great that there is someone who knows you so well to know what you'll choose or how you'll react to things. But are you robotic in that your preferences and choices are always the same? Should you not be allowed to make your choices yourself?

Anyone who feels they can speak up for you whenever you should be speaking for yourself is indirectly assuming control over your choices and taking away your voice.

#4 You Are Blamed for Everything That Doesn't Work

"We should have gotten the gold medal, but for your sluggishness." "We missed the show because you did not get to the bus station early." "The TV stopped working when you touched the remote." "I told you not to add any sauce to the noodles; now the noodles taste awful."

"Your dad left home the day you were born." "Your baby sister has not had anything to eat today because I gave you everything on me to get that weird book."

It's always you! Are you always the reason for things not working properly? Why should you be blamed for everything? If you are blamed for everything, you'll begin to feel something is wrong with you. If this persists, you'll drown in the sea of depression. You'll feel you are jinxed.

Hey! It's not about you; you just found yourself in the wrong relationship.

#5 You feel Ashamed of Yourself

"Girl, why is your dress so out of fashion? Don't you have a mirror at home?"

This might come out as a joke in a public place, but such a statement can so sorely hit you emotionally that every ounce of excitement you had before going for that event will dissipate. The next thing that will follow is you feel ashamed to mingle with anyone in that event; your self How can your friend do that to you?

It's a sign that that relationship is toxic.

#6 Your Interests Are Ridiculed

"You keep wasting your time throwing balls into the basket. My grandma throws the ball better than you. Go for something else." Ouch! That hurts. If that just came out from your friend, it came out really bad. It's an indication that your relationship is just about to get sore if it has not already.

#7 You Feel You are Not Good Enough

"Boy, you really put a lot into that show. But no matter how you try, you cannot just be good enough to be the lead role." What! That is just a way of saying, "Quit trying." It's a demoralizing statement that shouldn't be heard from someone we consider a friend or a close relative.

The list is not exhaustive. Any act that comes close to the ones I've listed indicates an unhealthy relationship.

How to End Unhealthy Relationships

First, you must admit that any relationship making you feel small and damaging your self-esteem is not good for you! This admittance should create enough reason to stop such a relationship.

Although there is no universal way to end unhealthy relationships, since the experience varies from person to person, I can suggest basic things that can be done to be free from such relationships.

Now, have you had enough toxicity in that relationship? Are you ready to take a break? Follow these basic steps:

1. Give Excuses to Withdraw

To withdraw gradually is to begin to reduce your time with people who abuse you in relationships. The more you spend time with such people or in a relationship, the higher the chances of getting hurt without caution. So, the most logical option is to reduce your time with such people.

Let it be gradual. When it's sudden, the other party might react more violently. So, you can start by creating some excuses as to why you cannot spend time with them. If you know they always embarrass you in public places, try to avoid going with them to any public place.

Reduce the line of communication. Don't always respond to their messages, and don't accept every invitation. At a point, you should have excuses for not attending any of the events they invite you to anymore.

Don't feel sorry or guilty for this, regardless of how the person involved reacts. You have to be radical and persistent in retrieving yourself from that relationship. It's only a matter of time before the emotional ties that bind you with them get severed.

If this doesn't work for you, try the next step

2. Get Busy With Other Things

The people who batter your emotions do so because you do things together. What if you get busy with other things – things that you know will take you away from those people. If it's in school, you can go for extracurricular activities that are different from what people do.

The most important thing is to detach from them by doing something different from what they are doing. When you get busy with your new tasks, which take you away from them, they won't have the opportunity to talk to you or engage you in any activity.

3. Announce the Break!

For this, you can announce the break, which will take a lot of courage, or you can allow the previous, ongoing steps to help you announce the break. Whichever option you opt for, ensure the other party sees clearly that the relationship is winding down and it's dying a natural death.

If the other party is not getting the signals, boldly announce, "I quit!"

4. Take Time to Heal

This is very important for you. You cannot go into another relationship with battered emotions. So, give yourself time to heal. During this period, take time to reflect on the things that have been damaged.

During this time, you'll need to believe in yourself again that your voice counts and your opinion needs to be heard:

You chose the right hobby, and you are not doing it to be a pro, so start enjoying your hobby again;

You are not insignificant that no one can know you are in a room:

You are good enough for the role you played, and even though there is room for improvement, you can play the lead role some day;

Your choice of dress is just perfect for you; don't feel ashamed of how you appear in your dress;

Hey! You are not jinxed! You are not to blame for everything that goes wrong.

I encourage you to go over this again at your own pace until you are sure you can walk with your shoulders high without shame or guilt. With that, you'll be ready to take on new relationships.

5. Turn Your Back to the Past and Look Forward

One of the things you must do while healing is to look away from your past experiences – the things you suffered, the things you lost, the opportunities you missed, etc., there is more for you in the future. Look to the future; better relationships and opportunities are awaiting you.

6. Get a Support Team Or Go for Therapy

This is a way to help you recover fully. It's better to have people who believe in you and always cheer you on around you. You can get such support from your relatives, friends, or from a therapist to help stabilize your emotions and help you move on completely from the toxic relationship.

7. Love Yourself Radically

This is the point I believe to be the icing on the cake. Unhealthy relationships have taught you to love yourself less because all you see is your defeat and failure. To recover, you must be unapologetic about loving yourself. You have every right to love yourself. Nobody can love you more than you. Love yourself radically. That is how to see the inner beauty in yourself.

Learning to Attract Positive People and Building a Relationship with Them

Like minds attract each other. If you have a positive mind, you can identify people who have a positive mind. Therefore, you must go through the previous healing and recovery phase before attempting to build new relationships.

Building a Positive Relationship is Possible. Before starting healthy relationships, you must believe it's possible. Though you have experienced an unhealthy one, you can have healthy ones, too.

Translate Your Experience to your Guide. Your experience in an unhealthy relationship can come in handy to guide you in your choice of a new relationship. Instead of allowing your negative experience to put it down, translate it into your guide in choosing new relationships.

Position Yourself Rightly. Nobody will notice you if you hide your face in the crowd. Step out and speak up. Laugh without anyone's consent. Volunteer to help whenever you can. That is how to position yourself for positive and healthy relationships.

Believe that there is still Goodness in People. Although you have experienced the worst things in people, this could make you skeptical about people. You can even find it hard to trust anyone again. But this will be one of your greatest hindrances to building a positive relationship. You cannot enjoy a new relationship if you keep harboring this thought. One of the signs that you are genuinely healing is when you can trust people again.

There are still good people out there. Don't be suspicious of people. If you follow the previous steps, you'll not go wrong.

Building Healthy Relationships Worksheet

This exercise helps you realize that sometimes, building healthy relationships starts with working on yourself. With this exercise, you'll identify ways to act in a relationship and how to find wholeness within yourself and become a better partner.

1. List out the emotions you feel most frequently

_____

_____

_____

_____

_____

2. Are you aware of the root cause of these feelings? Do you think it might result from a current situation in your life?

_____

_____

_____

_____

_____

_____

3. How are these emotions influencing your interactions/relationships with others?

_____

_____

_____

_____

_____

_____

4. Who is that person in your life you need to engage in a conversation with to foster a healthier relationship?

_____

_____

_____

_____

_____

_____

5. What have you been avoiding bringing up or talking about in a conversation?

_____

_____

_____

_____

6. What topic do you hope doesn't ever come up in a conversation with your partner?

_____

_____

_____

_____

7. What issues do you think you should revisit in your relationship?

_____

_____

_____

_____

8. How do you think you can revisit this conversation in a productive and meaningful way?

_____

_____

_____

_____

9. What positive outcome do you expect from revisiting this conversation?

_____

_____

_____

_____

_____

CHAPTER 11

Embracing and Strengthening Your Inner Child for Improved Self-love

Meet Stanley. Stanley was a 14-year-old teenager when his self-esteem began to deflate. Anyone who knew Stanley before knew him as a loveable, cheerful, and fun-to-be-with teenager. In just a blink of an eye, Stanley became moody and quiet. He no longer wanted to mix with people; he preferred staying alone to hanging out with his friends. No one ever thought Stanley would become so sullen that he would not want to hang out, not even with his childhood friend.

His parents tried so hard but could not find out what took over their cheery son.

What really happened to Stanley?

I'll tell you what happened to Stanley in a moment, but should you identify with Stanley's story, this chapter was specifically designed for you. Should you know someone who experienced what Stanley experienced, you might need to get a copy of this book to them.

So, what happened to Stanley? Stanley went out with his friend over the weekend to play soccer. Stanley had a golden chance to score a goal for the side he played for, but he lost the opportunity. That was a serious loss, but not so serious because it was just a game to have fun. His teammates shouted, but it was not to criticize him. He clasped his fingers on his face in disappointment, but it was just one of the moments of the exciting game.

But suddenly, a voice from outside the field echoed all over the playing field. It was not just Stanley that heard it:

"You kick like chicken!"

That was all Stanley heard that turned him into a gloomy teenager. But has Stanley not heard worse? He would not have reacted the way he did if that statement had not reminded him of a moment like that in his childhood. That statement refreshed his memory of a hurtful moment from his childhood. His mood changed immediately; he went home reliving the childhood memory. It influenced all his actions and inactions from that moment on. He began to feel inadequate, inefficient, not good enough, and doubtful; his self-esteem was shattered just with one statement.

Is there an explanation for this? Yes, there is. There is a psychological term for the part of Stanley that was brought back to life; they call it the "inner child." Deshlee Ford described the inner child as that susceptible and vulnerable part of our being that was shaped throughout our earliest stages of development. When we grow up, we begin to experience the manifestations of the behaviors that were formed during those early stages. Some of those behaviors could result from emotional and psychological neglect, trauma, or any other form of pain. Although many of us try to bury those experiences and the behaviors they produce deep in our unconscious, they still find a way to pop up whenever something triggers them.

Stanley, just like many other young persons out there, and reading this book right now, found a way to bury that traumatic experience. But no matter how strong the shield you build to protect it, Thich Nha Hanh in his book *Reconciliation – Healing the Inner Child,* said that the shield will not end the experience; it'll only prolong it.

Who is the Inner Child?

A lot of psychologists acknowledged a renowned psychiatrist, Carl Jung, to have coined the term when explaining his theory on that part of every human personality that is not obvious to the eyes but it's an essential part of our being. In explaining Carl Jung's theory, Crystal Raypole said the inner child is a link to our past experiences, and it reminds us of our innocence, playfulness, and creativity, and the anticipation for a utopian future.

Another way to look at it's that your childhood years are your formative years. Whatever experiences you had as a child shapes your personality and perception about yourself and the world around you. In other words, if you had positive experiences as a child, you'll grow up having a positive mindset about yourself and the world around you. Likewise, the negative experiences produce negative effects on you.

This concept shows us that we all have an inner child, and none of us really grows beyond it. A healthy inner child appears joyful, playful, fun-to-be-with, and child-like, but an unhealthy inner child struggles even after childhood and beyond; this happens whenever an event or any other thing triggers the memories of past awful experiences.

Do you still find it difficult to believe you have an inner child?

Try reflecting using these questions:

· Have you ever felt like there is a child in you that wants to be loved, cared for, felt innocent, or just simply wonder at the beauty of creation?

· Have you felt like having the freedom of a child where you spread your wings and just fly?

· Are there moments you have felt like doing those playful, childish things you used to do as a child?

If you answered in the affirmative to the questions above, there is a child within you. And no matter how old you grow, that child will always want to express itself. You might try to play the hard and untouchable boy, but there is no denying the fact that there is a child within your hard shell that desires to be loved, pampered, and encouraged.

Think of any quality you can attach to a child – innocence, wonder, naivety, creativity, etc. – those are the things that your inner child is made up of. Take a moment to look inwardly through reflection and inquisitiveness; you'll meet your inner child somewhere there.

How Does the Inner Child Affect Your Self-Esteem?

Now that you understand who the inner child is, what is the connection between this child and your self-esteem?

Follow this list to learn a few ways your inner child influences your self-esteem:

A Secure Inner Child makes an accepted and respected person

Aletheia, a psychospiritual writer and author, said that safety is not just a physical phenomenon, it also touches on the emotional, psychological, and spiritual aspects of our being. Your inner child is not in the physical dimension but in the inner being where your emotion and psychology are elements to consider.

When you feel safe emotionally and psychologically, you feel respected and accepted. You don't feel pressured to live in certain ways to please a group of people. When your internal child feels this way, you have found an ambience that supports your personal growth and development without fearing what people might say or think about you.

An Insecure Inner Child makes a fear-prone person

Just the opposite of the first point, when you feel insecure emotionally around a certain set of people, you are most likely to always be afraid around them. This will make you lose your composure; sometimes, you stutter excessively, or your palm becomes sweaty. These reactions would not be necessary if your internal being didn't feel threatened by the presence of such people. At this point, it becomes obvious that your self-esteem has been deflated.

An Abused Inner Child Makes an Ashamed Person

You can relate to this point if you have been abused emotionally at any point in your life. Virtually all forms of abuse reduce the victim to the background where they live in shame and never have the confidence to raise their heads among their pairs. They feel beaten and defeated. Some others carry the guilt of their experience with them for some time till they get help.

With the guilt, they feel sentenced to a life of shame and ridicule. They come to this conclusion without ever saying a word to anyone. They just curl up inwardly, but it will be obvious in their physical actions that something has tampered with their perspective about themselves.

A Crushed Inner Child Makes a Pessimistic Person

Imagine you are crushed inwardly through a series of events like failure in certain subjects, failure to meet the school standard, failure to be ever good enough for your parents, etc. If this myriad of failures continues, your inner child will feel crushed and defeated. You'll find it difficult to be positive about life or take on new challenges because you have failed so much to be excited about anything in life.

Pessimism is a symptom of low self-esteem. When you are told repeatedly that you are not good at certain things, it settles in your subconscious. The result is that you'll be pessimistic about attempting anything because you have been told you cannot do it.

A Loved Inner Child Makes a Confident Person

Love is the environment that breeds confidence in people. When people feel loved, they don't feel small about themselves. They go everywhere acting confidently without an iota of doubt about their identity or what they are capable of doing.

When you feel loved, you feel good about yourself. You'll see no reason to doubt yourself because you are in an environment that nurtures you with care, attention, encouragement, the right counsel, great criticism, etc.

How to Revive Your Inner Child

No one is truly hopeless until they take their final breath. As long as there is breath in your nostrils, you are not hopeless. You can rediscover your inner beauty. You can live the life of your dreams. You can heal!

How?

Step 1: Admittance

The first and most vital step is to consciously admit that you have an inner child that has shaped your perception of yourself and the world around you. If left unattended, it will keep influencing your perception into adulthood.

The earlier you admit its existence, the better for your personal healing and recovery.

Step 2: Embrace It

An embrace here is not the literal, physical demonstration. It's a figurative description to show affection and accept your inner child.

Every child thrives amid affection and acceptance. Your inner child won't need anything lesser. Don't just stop at admitting its existence; embrace it. It was denied such affection during childhood, but you can give your inner child a different feel of experience by showing it so much affection, and not just once. You must do it continuously till you are soaked in an atmosphere of love.

How do you embrace your inner child, you say?

Think of such words you longed to hear as a child, but you got the cruel opposite of those.

Tell your inner child, "I love you," "Don't get too anxious, we're in this together," "C'mon! You did great just now."

In this instance, you are alone speaking to yourself – the younger version of yourself. You'll feel a sense of peace and comfort internally when you do this. Yes! That is your inner child soaking in the embrace.

Step 3: Reflect and Revamp

This step will take time, but much more, you'll need to confront yourself with an honest truth without giving much heed to the hurt. If you do, this could be the last hurt your inner child will feel in this regard.

In reflecting, you'll take a journey back into the past to begin to trace where and how your inner child got injured. Let's use Jeremy Sutton's reflection timeline as an example. With it you can glimpse what to do when taking steps back in time to your early years.

Think of something that happened when you were age five, age eight, age nine, age ten, age fifteen, etc. Yours might not even be those years; it could be different. However, it's just to aid your reflection.

The purpose of this is not to drag you back into the mud of hurt but to help you administer the right solution for your context. It'll also help you to revamp the inner child's experiences. This takes us to the next step.

Step 4: Pay Attention!

After reflecting and tracing the history and source of the emotional traits you exhibit, there cannot be revamping until you begin to pay attention to the emotional responses you exhibit when similar actions take place now.

For instance, when your mom and dad divorced when you were just five, you felt broken. Now, what similar action takes place now that makes you feel broken again?

Ability to identify this will help you to do the next thing.

Step 5: Speak & Set Boundaries

Now you have identified the things that influence the reaction of the inner child in certain ways, you know that the inner child has a need in that regard. So, you start by addressing the need by speaking to it to put it on a notice that such emotional reactions can be controlled.

Then you go ahead to set boundaries internally to mitigate the kind of occurrences that trigger such responses.

Step 6: Journaling

Journaling is a great way to translate your emotions, thoughts, feelings, and experiences into words. It takes a degree of burden off your mind.

Journaling is a great way to reflect; you can go over your actions and identify what you should have done better or cut off altogether.

Healing Your Inner Child Worksheet

This exercise explores your developmental years and focuses on how key or specific events during your childhood cause challenges in your adult life. In this exercise, you will mention the emotional impact this situation had on you and the intensity of this emotion from 1-10.

Afterwards, you will have a conversation with your inner child about your understanding of the situation then and how hurt you really were. With this, you can help your inner child react to situations better and let them know that it isn't the same as back then.

Approximate age	Describe What happened	Emotion felt and intensity of emotion (1-10)

1. Choosing one of these events, what secrets are you holding about this scenario?

_____

_____

_____

_____

2. What deep hurts do you carry about this event?

_____

_____

_____

_____

3. Concerning this situation, what will your inner child like to say to you as an adult right now?

_____

_____

_____

_____

4. What current situations elicit this same emotional response from you, and how does your inner child respond?

_____

_____

_____

_____

5. How do you help your inner child know the situation is now different while being compassionate about it?

_____

_____

_____

_____

Bonus Resources

Bonus #1: 200 Affirmations for Self-Compassion

It's the repetition of affirmations that leads to belief. And once that belief becomes a deep conviction, things begin to happen.

- Muhammad Ali

I spoke about talking to yourself in the previous chapter to heal and recover. Now, it's time to practice one of the things you have learned. Don't be ashamed of affirming any of these statements to yourself. This is you talking to *you* because you are about to experience a fundamental transformation in your earthly journey.

Now affirm to yourself or remind yourself of things about yourself with confidence:

1. I deserve to be loved.

2. I deserve respect.

3. I deserve honor.

4. I deserve to be heard.

5. I am valuable.

6. I am not a liability.

7. I am significant.

8. I am good enough.

9. I am proud of who I am becoming.

10. I am a beautiful being.

11. I appreciate my uniqueness.

12. I am confident.

13. I am not timid.

14. I am kind and patient with myself.

15. I am compassionate to myself.

16. I understand my growth experience.

17. I permit myself to grow steadily

18. Everyone makes mistakes; I am not exempted.

19. My mistakes don't define me.

20. I forgive myself for my past mistakes.

21. I am not stuck in the past.

22. My past is not my final destination.

23. There are better days ahead of me.

24. I am happy with the process of becoming.

25. I am patient with the process.

26. I love who I am becoming.

27. I step out to live life to the fullest today.

28. I learn from my past mistakes.

29. I get better daily.

30. I admit I am not perfect.

31. I accept my imperfections, but I am getting better.

32. When I don't do things right, I am not hard on myself.

33. I am flexible in adapting to changes.

34. I am not dogmatic in applying recovery methods.

35. I treat myself with love and understanding.

36. I always get back up whenever I fall.

37. I am not a weakling.

38. I don't live on the sympathy of people.

39. I am my loudest cheerleader.

40. I appreciate the commitment I put into getting better.

41. I am allowing myself enough time to get better.

42. I am not emotional about what people say to me.

43. I don't allow negative criticisms to get me down.

44. I utilize every criticism for my personal well-being

45. I am not a people-pleaser.

46. I can decide what is good for me.

47. I have a strong mind.

48. I make the right choices for myself.

49. I don't sacrifice my happiness for other people's happiness.

50. I deserve to be happy.

51. I love myself unapologetically.

52. Self-compassion is my new norm.

53. I practice self-love daily.

54. I don't need anyone's permission to care for myself.

55. As I care for myself, I see my inner beauty rise.

56. It is healthy for me to take time to heal.

57. I am healed from past unhealthy relationships.

58. It is okay to let go of toxic relationships

59. I am grateful for the experiences I had in past relationships.

60. I am the best friend for me.

61. I am my best gist-mate.

62. I am entitled to me time.

63. I am open to new relationships.

64. I only see goodness in people.

65. I am a good friend.

66. I bring value into my relationships.

67. My opinion counts.

68. My thoughts and words are powerful.

69. I attract positive friends only.

70. I am surrounded by healthy friends.

71. I say positive things only to myself.

72. I am intelligent.

73. I am smart.

74. I am diligent.

75. My looks don't define me.

76. I am beautiful.

77. I am not ashamed of my looks.

78. I am grateful for my shape.

79. I have a great body.

80. I don't feel pressure to impress anyone.

81. I have the right to look good.

82. I am content with my status.

83. I am happy with my birth origin

84. I am gorgeous.

85. I am talented.

86. I am grateful for my abilities.

87. I always make the best use of my time.

88. I am committed to honing my skills.

89. I am not mediocre.

90. I excel at what I do.

91. I am not jinxed.

92. I am not to blame for other people's failures.

93. I am free of guilt.

94. I don't feel sorry for offenses I don't commit.

95. I take responsibility for my mistakes.

96. I am not a crybaby.

97. I am stable emotionally.

98. My friends and family love and respect me.

99. I let go of negative self-beliefs.

100. I cultivate love around me.

101. I am whole.

102. I am healed.

103. I am secure in myself

104. I am focused.

105. I am purposeful.

106. I am powerful.

107. I am healthy.

108. I am progressive.

109. I am forward-thinking.

110. I am a force to reckon with.

111. I am not sorry about my state.

112. I am not sad about my circumstances.

113. I am beaming with hope.

114. I am not angry with myself.

115. I have control over my emotions.

116. My emotions don't dictate actions.

117. I don't react with bitterness.

118. I am not a product of hatred.

119. I don't spread hatred.

120. I am always happy.

121. I am excited about each day.

122. I always rise up full of hope.

123. I am better than the hate I received.

124. I am kind.

125. I am generous in giving love.

126. I am grateful for the opportunity to live happily.

127. I face every challenge cheerfully.

128. I give love for bitterness.

129. I see beauty in myself.

130. I cultivate my inner beauty.

131. I am committed to myself.

132. I am growing stronger.

133. I am better than I was yesterday.

134. I get better daily.

135. I am not afraid of new challenges.

136. I take advantage of opportunities to get better.

137. I am excited about the new me.

138. My shield of ego is broken.

139. I have a free mind towards all people.

140. I have a healthy relationship with everyone.

141. I am creative.

142. I am full of self-confidence.

143. I am influential.

144. I can do anything I set my mind on.

145. I have the ability to create the life I desire.

146. I am just what I need to succeed.

147. I am at peace internally.

148. My inner being is secured.

149. My inner child is healed.

150. My inner child basks in love.

151. I don't feel bad about myself.

152. My daily events don't decide my mood.

153. My emotions are not controlled by circumstances.

154. I am in charge of my life.

155. I don't feel sorry for setting boundaries.

156. I emit love and goodness.

157. I respect other people's unit paths.

158. I am courageous.

159. I am not a coward.

160. I embrace all my fears.

161. I dare things that got me down before

162. My self-worth grows daily.

163. My self-esteem keeps growing daily.

164. I believe in my skills.

165. I have a great personality.

166. I am capable of doing great things.

167. I am magnificent.

168. I deserve the good things I have.

169. I am not inadequate.

170. I don't sag my head in shame.

171. I am not anxious.

172. I am not intimidated by the progress of others.

173. I am content with who I am.

174. Every day is a beautiful day.

175. I celebrate my accomplishments.

176. I matter.

177. My existence is not coincidental.

178. I live for a purpose.

179. I translate my failures into learning tools.

180. I am optimistic.

181. I am incapable of hatred or bitterness.

182. I am my priority.

183. I have great dreams.

184. My dreams are not impossible.

185. I am capable of achieving my dreams.

186. I don't compete with others.

187. I am my competition.

188. I run at my pace.

189. I am at peace with my success.

190. I am consistent.

191. I am not erratic.

192. I am healthy, vibrant, and smart.

193. I have a vibrant mind.

194. I emit positive energy to people around me.

195. My inner beauty shines for all to see.

196. My self-worth rises in value.

197. I am my best investment.

198. I am capable of loving.

199. I am not rigid to change.

200. I am allergic to bitterness.

Bonus #2: Great Morning Habits to Kick-start Self-love and Self-compassion on a Daily Basis

The morning is an amazing time of the day. I have it on good authority that when you have a good start, you're very likely to enjoy the rest of it. As we bring this mental upgrade software to a close, it's important to show you how to use the morning routine hack to get your self-esteem gauge rising and stuff.

The other day, I saw a video from Bright Side about Millionaire Morning Habits. In there, they made a big deal out of small habits like waking up early and exercising. Well, sorry if you're not a morning person, but they're right. I get it if you like to stay in bed a bit longer than 5 am, but as it is, we're going to have to meet up in the middle somewhere. Because great self-esteem doesn't come cheap, and one of the prices is making sure you start your day on the right foot.

So what are these golden habits? If you're still tongue-in-cheek, you need to stop it now. I promise you that these habits will change your life.

1. Move your wake-up time backward by thirty minutes. Ideally, we recommend getting up by 5:30 am. Where's your alarm clock now?

2. Try stretching in the morning, say for five minutes. Simple stretches are just enough to get you going.

3. Water. Bet you didn't see that one coming. Drink some water. It doesn't have to be much.

4. Get the hygiene thing going early enough; bath, shave, brush your teeth, style your hair, the works.

5. Say positive things to yourself while you're in the bathroom. This

is where affirmations can come in nicely.

6. Get yourself a good, sumptuous, non-oily breakfast.

7. Music–good, affirmative music in the mornings will also do wonders for you.

8. Wear clothes you're absolutely comfortable in. Make sure they're not too loose or too tight.

9. Your commuting time should be spent learning something new– watching an educational video on YouTube or reading a book chapter. Leadership, mental resilience, boundary setting, and confidence building are examples of useful topics you can read about.

10. Have a to-do list that will guide your approach to each day's tasks.

11. Send gratitude emails or texts in the mornings. Just reach out to one or two persons who have been helping make life more interesting and say thank you.

12. Cold showers! They do wonders for jolting you to life and making you feel good.

13. Incorporate five minutes of meditation into your morning. Using the meditation guides in this book, give it a try.

14. Try also to give minutes of visualization. Imagine yourself as that person you dream to be.

15. Make your bed before you leave home. If you work from home, make your bed before you start working.

16. Always do a quick declutter in the mornings or every other morning. Rearrange the shelf, return the hat to its position, etc.

17.   And finally, on our list, what's a great morning without some good music? Play music you love before heading out.

You don't have to begin them all at once. Gentleness is a strategy that gets these things truly working for you. Don't be hard on yourself. Try it one at a time and master them gradually. It might seem like the hardest thing you've been asked to do since you started reading this book, but if you follow through, you're going to have wonderful self-esteem to thank. You'll be in love with the new version of you that'll emerge.

Bonus #3: Self-Compassion Worksheet

We often treat our friends better than we treat ourselves in the same scenario. This exercise focuses on helping you start treating yourself as you would a good friend.

1. First, consider instances when a close friend is genuinely struggling or feels awful about themselves. In this circumstance, what would you say to your friend (especially when you're at your best)? Please record your regular actions and words, as well as how you speak to your friends.

_____

_____

_____

_____

_____

_____

2. Now consider instances in which you had self-doubt or struggled. In these circumstances, how do you generally reply to yourself? Please record your regular actions, words, and tone of voice when speaking to yourself.

_____

_____

_____

_____

_____

_____

_____

3. Have you noticed a distinction? If so, consider why. What motivating motives or anxieties cause you to treat others and yourself so differently?

_____

_____

_____

_____

_____

_____

4. Take note of a current situation or circumstance making you doubt yourself or struggle and your initial response to this.

_____

_____

_____

_____

_____

_____

5. Now talk to yourself as if you were talking to your friend in a calmer, kind way, and employ how you speak to your friends.

_____

_____

_____

_____

_____

6. Please describe how you think things may change if you treat yourself the same way you treat a close friend when you're going through a difficult time.

_____

_____

_____

_____

_____

_____

7. Whenever you are judgmental or overly critical of yourself in the future, remember to reframe your dialogue to be more compassionate and supportive.

Conclusion

I think we know each other pretty well at this point, right? So, you'd say that we can feel comfortable around each other, right?

So you won't mind if I do what I'm about to do, right? You won't mind if I burst out in a cheer and tell you congratulations for making it this far? No?

OK great! Here goes!

Yay! Look at you! You made it to the end of the book! Way to go! *does a star cartwheel* Don't ask me what a star cartwheel looks like, thanks. Haha.

We've come a long way here. We've started from the very beginning; we went to the basics of self-love, we saw how self-love was the missing link to happiness. The big reveal for me was the part that talked about how not practicing self-love could make for a sad life. If you don't know what I mean, check chapter one for the signs that show that self-love is missing from your life. On the other hand, we also saw what life looks like when you're tight with self-love, and I gotta say, boy does self-love win every time.

Next up, self-love vs radical self-love, is there a difference? Yep. Radical self-love is about fighting to choose yourself in a world that says self-love is selfish. It means doing the hard work needed to grow and heal. Sadly if you don't love yourself, your self-esteem is probably not doing great either. The great news is that once you start to love yourself more, your self-esteem and self-compassion start to go up too. Talk about three for the price of one, huh?

Self-compassion isn't spoken of very often, but it plays an important role in rescuing your self-love and reviving your self-esteem. Thankfully, you learned the exact steps needed to start practicing self-compassion as soon as possible. Self-forgiveness goes hand in hand with self-compassion, so we had to take a closer look at it as well. I showed you all the possible reasons and probable thought patterns that were responsible for low self-esteem. Reframing these thought patterns was the next thing to learn, and we saw all the possible ways to challenge and think positively. If you've succeeded in understanding that part of this book, you've learned an invaluable life lesson that will stick with you forever.

We moved on to the juicier parts of the book, where we looked at how to practice self-forgiveness and practiced a few awesome mindful breathing exercises. I pulled out my secret weapon and taught you how to journal like a pro.

We went into the deeper aspects of effective self-care and looked at the fact that forgiving other people was the logical next step after forgiving ourselves. We looked at the nitty-gritty of forgiving other people, and we busted some assumptions about forgiveness. The most insightful part was the fact that forgiving someone didn't mean that you approve of what they did, rather forgiveness is solely for your benefit. So, it doesn't matter what they said or did; you're already in the right of way.

Since we're in the mood to bring this whole house down, we looked at people-pleasing and why it was bad for everyone involved. We laid out practical steps for overcoming it as well as for taking your power back. We considered everything involved in training oneself to become more self-compassionate. The bonuses included in the book will go a long way to support and encourage you, plus you can refer back to them any time you feel down or need some encouragement. You have to agree with me at this point that my goal for writing this book was to make sure that you get served—in a good way.

You are deserving of happiness. You are lovable and relevant. Spend each day from now on living this reality, and don't ever listen to anyone or any situation that tries to tell you otherwise.

I've shared. Now it's your turn to share what you learned and what part of the book resonated most with you. I'm waiting for you in the reviews section on Amazon. I'll really love to hear your comments.

References

Aletheia (2022, May 20).

25 Signs You Have a Wounded Inner Child (and How to Heal). https://lonerwolf.com/feeling-safe-inner-child/

Ford, D. (2021, July 16).

Reparenting Your Inner Child: Ways to Encourage Therapeutic Dialogue. https://www.stepupformentalhealth.org/reparenting-your-inner-child/

Hanh, T. N. (2006).

Reconciliation: Healing the Inner Child (first edition). Parallax Press.

Raypole, C. (2019, December 4).

How to Stop People-Pleasing (and Still Be Nice). https://www.healthline.com/health/people-pleaser

Raypole, C. (2020, June 26).

Finding and Getting to Know Your Inner Child. https://www.healthline.com/health/people-pleaser

Sutton, J. (2022, October 8).

Inner Child Healing: 35 Practical Tools for Growing Beyond Your Past. https://positivepsychology.com/inner-child-healing/

Cornish, M. A., & Wade, N. G. (2015).

A therapeutic model of self-forgiveness with intervention strategies for counselors. Journal of Counseling & Development, 93(1), 96–104. https://doi.org/10.1002/j.1556-6676.2015.00185.x

Chen, Y. F, Huang X.Y, Chien C. H, Cheng J. F (2016).

The Effectiveness of Diaphragmatic Breathing Relaxation Training for Reducing Anxiety. Perspect Psychiatr Care. 2017 Oct;53(4):329-336. doi:10.1111/ppc.12184.PMID:27553981.

Downey, C., & Crummy, A. (2022).

The impact of childhood trauma on children's wellbeing and adult behavior. European Journal of Trauma & Dissociation, 6(1), 100237. https://doi.org/10.1016/j.ejtd.2021.100237

Jerath R, Crawford MW, Barnes VA, Harden K (2015).

Self-regulation of breathing as a primary treatment for anxiety. Appl Psychophysiol Biofeedback. 2015 Jun;40(2):107-15. doi: 10.1007/s10484-015-9279-8. PMID: 25869930.

Krause, N., Shaw, B. A., Cairney, J. (2004).

A descriptive epidemiology of lifetime trauma and the physical health status of older adults. Psychology and Aging, 19(4), 637–648. https://doi.org/10.1037/0882-7974.19.4.637

Malhotra V, Bharshankar R, Ravi N, Bhagat O. L (2021).

Acute Effects on Heart Rate Variability during Slow Deep Breathing. Mymensingh Med J. 2021 Jan;30(1):208-213. PMID: 33397876.

Wiersma J. E, Hovens J. G, van Oppen P, Giltay E. J, van Schaik D. J, Beekman A. T, Penninx B. W (2009).

The importance of childhood trauma and childhood life events for chronicity of depression in adults. J Clin Psychiatry. 2009 Jul;70(7):983-9. DOI: 10.4088/jcp.08m04521. PMID: 19653975.

Ackerman, C. E. (2022, September 8).

Cognitive distortions: 22 examples & worksheets (& PDF). PositivePsychology.com. Retrieved September 16, 2022, from https://positivepsychology.com/cognitive-distortions/#common-cognitive-distortions

Buckley, D. (2022, August 16).

What is cognitive reframing and why do therapists use it? BetterHelp. Retrieved September 16, 2022, from https://www.betterhelp.com/advice/therapy/what-is-cognitive-reframing-and-why-do-therapists-use-it/#:~:text=An%20example%20of%20cognitive%20reframing,being%20able%20to%20maintain%20friendships.

References

Casabianca, S. S. (2022, January 11).

15 cognitive distortions to blame for your negative thinking. Psych Central. Retrieved September 18, 2022, from https://psychcentral.com/lib/cognitive-distortions-negative-thinking#conclusions

Good Therapy. (2015).

20 cognitive distortions and how they affect your life - goodtherapy.org therapy blog. Good Therapy. Retrieved September 16, 2022, from https://www.google.com/amp/s/www.goodtherapy.org/blog/20-cognitive-distortions-and-how-they-affect-your-life-0407154/amp/

Hadiah. (2022, September 11).

What causes cognitive distortions? Ineffable Living. Retrieved September 16, 2022, from https://ineffableliving.com/stop-cognitive-distortions-and-overcome-depression/

Hartney, E. (2021, November).

10 cognitive distortions you'll learn about in therapy. Verywell Mind. Retrieved September 18, 2022, from https://www.verywellmind.com/ten-cognitive-distortions-identified-in-cbt-22412#toc-labeling

Naoumidis, A. (2019).

Thinking traps: 12 cognitive distortions that are hijacking your brain. Mindset Health. Retrieved September 18, 2022, from https://www.mindsethealth.com/matter/thinking-traps-cognitive-distortions

Star, K. (2022).

Why do people jump to conclusions? Verywell Mind. Retrieved 2022, from https://www.verywellmind.com/jumping-to-conclusions-2584181

Timm, H. (2021, November 12).

The fallacy of Change (a cognitive distortion). Courageous Mindful. Retrieved September 18, 2022, from https://courageousandmindful.com/the-fallacy-of-change-a-cognitive-distortion/#:~:text=How%20To%20Challenge%20The%20Fallacy,they%20respond%20to%20specific%20situations.

Wetter, M. G., & Bailey , E. (2016).

What went right - reframe your thinking for a happier now. Hazelden Information & Education.

Neff, K. D. (2009). The Role of Self-Compassion in Development:

A Healthier Way to Relate to Oneself. Human development, 52(4), 211-214. https://doi.org/10.1159/000215071

Krieger T, Altenstein D, Bättig I, Doerig N, Holtforth MG.

Self-compassion in depression: associations with depressive symptoms, rumination, and avoidance in depressed outpatients. Behav Ther. 2013 Sep;44(3):501-13. doi: 10.1016/j.beth.2013.04.004. Epub 2013 Apr 18. PMID: 23768676.

Körner, A., Coroiu, A., Copeland, L., Gomez-Garibello, C., Albani, C., Zenger, M., & Brähler, E. (2015).

The Role of Self-Compassion in Buffering Symptoms of Depression in the General Population. PLOS ONE, 10(10), e0136598. https://doi.org/10.1371/journal.pone.0136598

Nguyen, D. T., Wright, E. P., Dedding, C., Pham, T. T., & Bunders, J. (2019).

Low Self-Esteem and Its Association With Anxiety, Depression, and Suicidal Ideation in Vietnamese Secondary School Students: A Cross-Sectional Study. Frontiers in Psychiatry. https://doi.org/10.3389/fpsyt.2019.00698

Baumeister R.F., Campbell J.D., Krueger J.I., Vohs K.D.

Does high self-esteem cause better performance, interpersonal success, happiness, or healthier lifestyles? Psychological Science in the Public Interest. 2003;4(1):1–44.